THE
NIGHTMARE
FACTORY

BASED ON THE STORIES OF

Thomas Ligotti

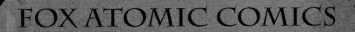

FOX ATOMIC COMICS

Editor in Chief

R. ERIC LIEB

Editor

HEIDI MacDONALD

Designer

SYMON CHOW

SPECIAL THANKS

Thomas Ligotti, Peter Rice,
John Hegeman, Debbie Liebling,
Duncan Macdonald, Karen Crawford,
Andre Costa de Sousa, Miki Reynolds,
Nancy Kim, Fox Atomic Online,
Kyle Franke, Jimmy Palmiotti,
Hope Innelli, Jeremy Cesarec,
Kris Oprisko, Tim Bradstreet,
Richard Starkings, Jimmy Betancourt,
Albert Deschesne, Michael Shlain,
Francesca Mannoni, Maria Medina

The Nightmare Factory

Fox Atomic Comics

An Imprint of HarperCollins*Publishers*

ISBN: 978-0-06-124353-0   ISBN-10: 0-06-124353-1

❖

First Edition

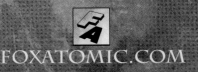

FOXATOMIC.COM

Table of Contents

cover art by ASHLEY WOOD

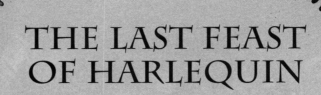

THE LAST FEAST
OF HARLEQUIN

In many ways, *The Last Feast of Harlequin* has all the earmarks of a pastiche of the works of H. P. Lovecraft. Indeed, his footprints can be found running throughout the narrative, which includes a protagonist who is a man of science, an architecturally bizarre town that is off the beaten track, a cult that practices cryptic rituals, and, supremely, a monster. All of these are stalwart elements of Lovecraft's horror tales. But a deviation from the Lovecraftian creeps into *The Last Feast of Harlequin* in its focus on the narrator's psychology.

While the spokesmen for Lovecraft's horrors all become mentally unsound by the end of their respective misadventures, the protagonist of *The Last Feast of Harlequin* is something of a basket case to begin with. And from there he only gets worse as he steps into a nightmare that both echoes and aggravates his despairing psychology. By profession, the central figure of *The Last Feast of Harlequin* is an anthropologist, one who suffers from what the psychiatric literature designates as seasonal affective disorder. This affliction comes upon its victim, so goes the theory, in the winter months when daylight is most meager and darkness most long. Hence the climax of the story takes place during the longest night of the year in a northern town.

Another departure in *The Last Feast of Harlequin* from the standard Lovecraftian framework is the festival held by the town of Mirocaw during the high point of winter, when sunny moods are inclined to flag. In the manner of other holidays around the time of the winter solstice, Mirocaw's feast is appointed to take place when night rolls in early and leaves late. The drama of the tale is therefore one of denial and repression on the part of the Mirocavians when confronted with forces inimical to their lives in particular and to all life in general. The manner in which Mirocaw evades a plague of depression lies in the willingness of people to turn their eyes away from the darkness and put on a happy face. As bad luck would have it, however, there are other forces in the town that have dark plans of their own.

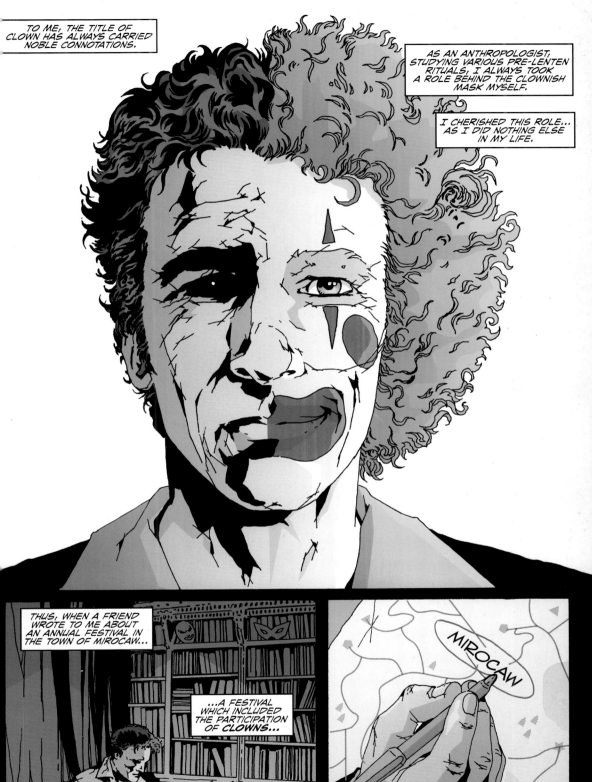

TO ME, THE TITLE OF CLOWN HAS ALWAYS CARRIED NOBLE CONNOTATIONS.

AS AN ANTHROPOLOGIST, STUDYING VARIOUS PRE-LENTEN RITUALS, I ALWAYS TOOK A ROLE BEHIND THE CLOWNISH MASK MYSELF.

I CHERISHED THIS ROLE... AS I DID NOTHING ELSE IN MY LIFE.

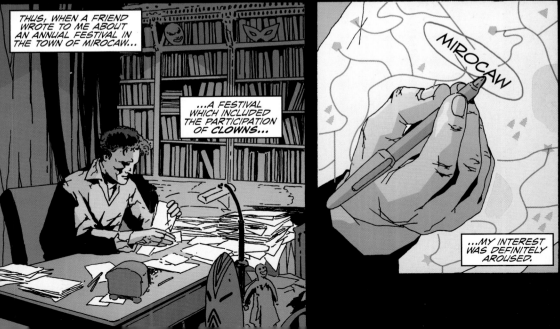

THUS, WHEN A FRIEND WROTE TO ME ABOUT AN ANNUAL FESTIVAL IN THE TOWN OF MIROCAW...

...A FESTIVAL WHICH INCLUDED THE PARTICIPATION OF CLOWNS...

MIROCAW

...MY INTEREST WAS DEFINITELY AROUSED.

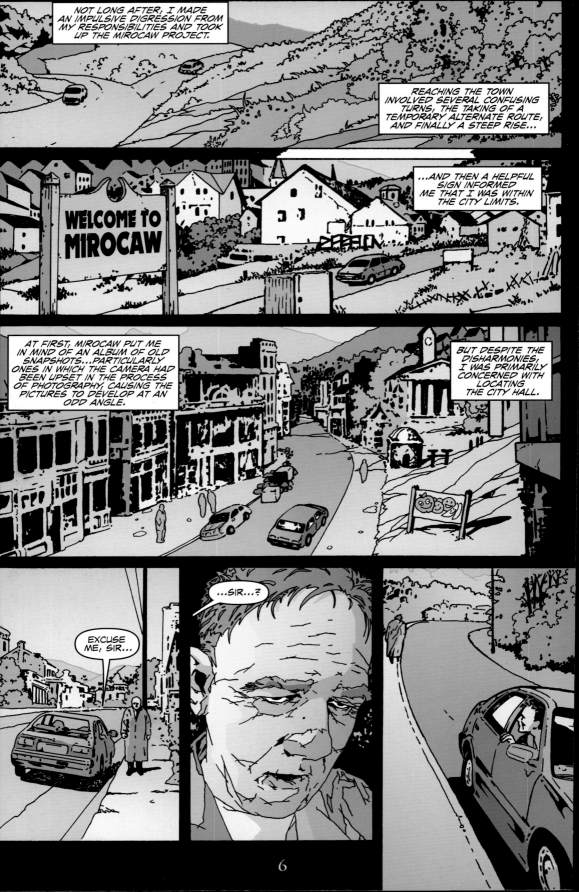

NOT LONG AFTER, I MADE AN IMPULSIVE DIGRESSION FROM MY RESPONSIBILITIES AND TOOK UP THE MIROCAW PROJECT.

REACHING THE TOWN INVOLVED SEVERAL CONFUSING TURNS, THE TAKING OF A TEMPORARY ALTERNATE ROUTE, AND FINALLY A STEEP RISE...

...AND THEN A HELPFUL SIGN INFORMED ME THAT I WAS WITHIN THE CITY LIMITS.

WELCOME TO MIROCAW

AT FIRST, MIROCAW PUT ME IN MIND OF AN ALBUM OF OLD SNAPSHOTS...PARTICULARLY ONES IN WHICH THE CAMERA HAD BEEN UPSET IN THE PROCESS OF PHOTOGRAPHY, CAUSING THE PICTURES TO DEVELOP AT AN ODD ANGLE.

BUT DESPITE THE DISHARMONIES, I WAS PRIMARILY CONCERNED WITH LOCATING THE CITY HALL.

EXCUSE ME, SIR...

...SIR...?

6

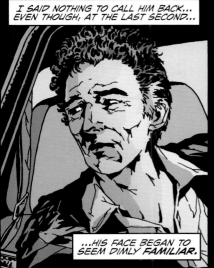

I SAID NOTHING TO CALL HIM BACK... EVEN THOUGH, AT THE LAST SECOND...

...HIS FACE BEGAN TO SEEM DIMLY *FAMILIAR*.

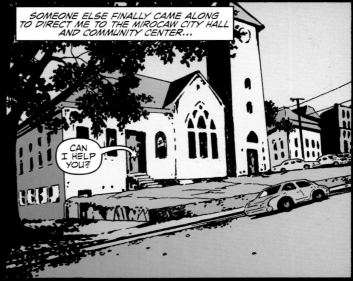

SOMEONE ELSE FINALLY CAME ALONG TO DIRECT ME TO THE MIROCAW CITY HALL AND COMMUNITY CENTER...

CAN I HELP YOU?

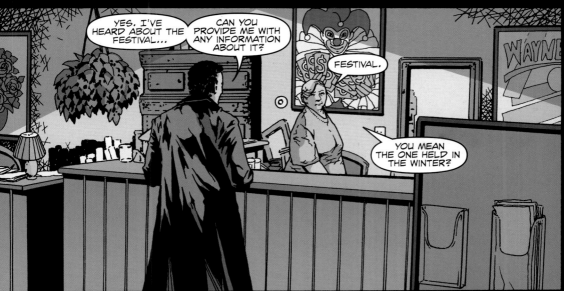

YES. I'VE HEARD ABOUT THE FESTIVAL...

CAN YOU PROVIDE ME WITH ANY INFORMATION ABOUT IT?

FESTIVAL.

YOU MEAN THE ONE HELD IN THE WINTER?

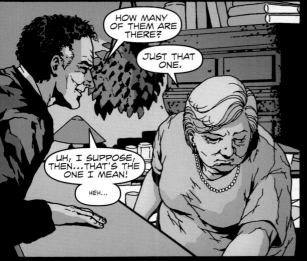

HOW MANY OF THEM ARE THERE?

JUST THAT ONE.

UH, I SUPPOSE, THEN...THAT'S THE ONE I MEAN!

HEH...

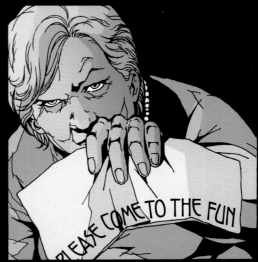

PLEASE COME TO THE FUN

PLEASE COME TO THE FUN
PARADES
STREET MASQUERADE
BANDS
THE WINTER RAFFLE
THE CORONATION OF
THE WINTER QUEEN
DEC. 19-21
IF YOU DON'T MIND MY ASKING...DON'T THESE DAYS SOMEWHAT CONFLICT WITH THE HOLIDAY SEASON?
IT'S JUST TRADITION.
IS THERE ANYTHING ELSE?
YES.
COULD YOU TELL ME IF THIS FESTIVAL HAS ANYTHING TO DO WITH CLOWNS?
YES, OF COURSE THERE ARE SOME PEOPLE IN...COSTUMES. MYSELF, I'VE NEVER...
THAT IS, YES. THERE ARE CLOWNS.
OF A SORT.

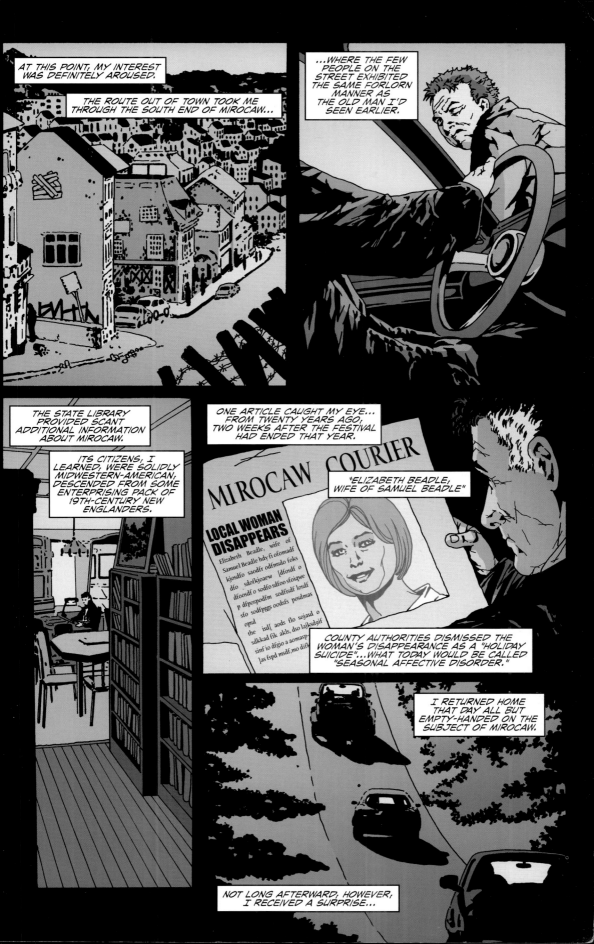

AT THIS POINT, MY INTEREST WAS DEFINITELY AROUSED.

THE ROUTE OUT OF TOWN TOOK ME THROUGH THE SOUTH END OF MIROCAW...

...WHERE THE FEW PEOPLE ON THE STREET EXHIBITED THE SAME FORLORN MANNER AS THE OLD MAN I'D SEEN EARLIER.

THE STATE LIBRARY PROVIDED SCANT ADDITIONAL INFORMATION ABOUT MIROCAW.

ITS CITIZENS, I LEARNED, WERE SOLIDLY MIDWESTERN-AMERICAN, DESCENDED FROM SOME ENTERPRISING PACK OF 19TH-CENTURY NEW ENGLANDERS.

ONE ARTICLE CAUGHT MY EYE... FROM TWENTY YEARS AGO, TWO WEEKS AFTER THE FESTIVAL HAD ENDED THAT YEAR.

MIROCAW COURIER

LOCAL WOMAN DISAPPEARS

Elizabeth Beadle, wife of Samuel Beadle hdy fi ofomadf kjosdfo saodfr odfmsdo foks dfo sdofkjoaew [dfoosdf o dfoosdf o sodfo sdfoo sfofqwe p dfpospodfm sodfisdf losdf sfo sodfpegs oodsfs posdmas opsd the isdf[aods flo sojasd o sdkkad fik akls, dso lajksdgif sinf io dfgio a aomasp Jas fspd msdf,mo difi

"ELIZABETH BEADLE, WIFE OF SAMUEL BEADLE"

COUNTY AUTHORITIES DISMISSED THE WOMAN'S DISAPPEARANCE AS A "HOLIDAY SUICIDE"...WHAT TODAY WOULD BE CALLED "SEASONAL AFFECTIVE DISORDER."

I RETURNED HOME THAT DAY ALL BUT EMPTY-HANDED ON THE SUBJECT OF MIROCAW.

NOT LONG AFTERWARD, HOWEVER, I RECEIVED A SURPRISE...

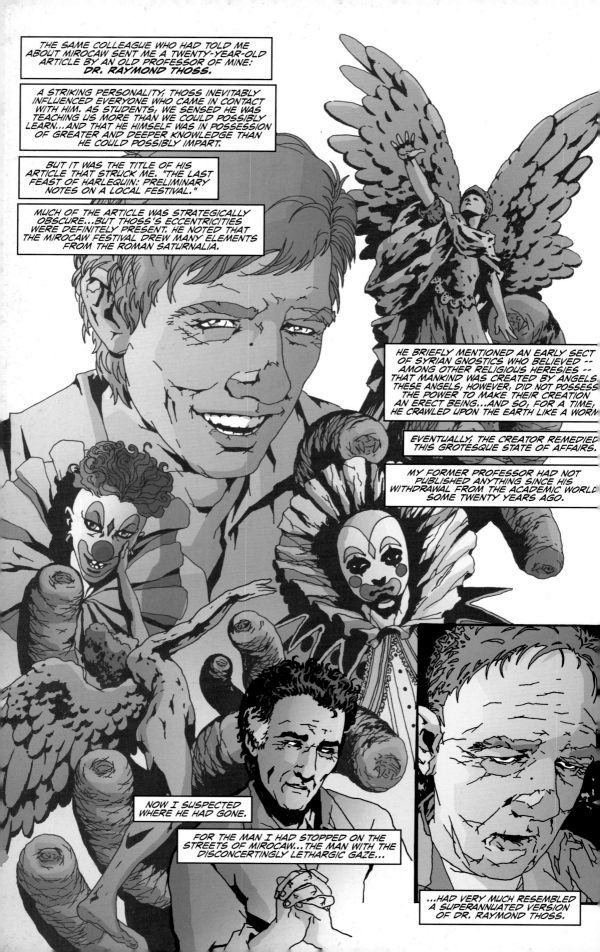

THE SAME COLLEAGUE WHO HAD TOLD ME ABOUT MIROCAW SENT ME A TWENTY-YEAR-OLD ARTICLE BY AN OLD PROFESSOR OF MINE: **DR. RAYMOND THOSS.**

A STRIKING PERSONALITY, THOSS INEVITABLY INFLUENCED EVERYONE WHO CAME IN CONTACT WITH HIM. AS STUDENTS, WE SENSED HE WAS TEACHING US MORE THAN WE COULD POSSIBLY LEARN...AND THAT HE HIMSELF WAS IN POSSESSION OF GREATER AND DEEPER KNOWLEDGE THAN HE COULD POSSIBLY IMPART.

BUT IT WAS THE TITLE OF HIS ARTICLE THAT STRUCK ME. "THE LAST FEAST OF HARLEQUIN: PRELIMINARY NOTES ON A LOCAL FESTIVAL."

MUCH OF THE ARTICLE WAS STRATEGICALLY OBSCURE...BUT THOSS'S ECCENTRICITIES WERE DEFINITELY PRESENT. HE NOTED THAT THE MIROCAW FESTIVAL DREW MANY ELEMENTS FROM THE ROMAN SATURNALIA.

HE BRIEFLY MENTIONED AN EARLY SECT OF SYRIAN GNOSTICS WHO BELIEVED -- AMONG OTHER RELIGIOUS HERESIES -- THAT MANKIND WAS CREATED BY ANGELS. THESE ANGELS, HOWEVER, DID NOT POSSESS THE POWER TO MAKE THEIR CREATION AN ERECT BEING...AND SO, FOR A TIME, HE CRAWLED UPON THE EARTH LIKE A WORM.

EVENTUALLY, THE CREATOR REMEDIED THIS GROTESQUE STATE OF AFFAIRS.

MY FORMER PROFESSOR HAD NOT PUBLISHED ANYTHING SINCE HIS WITHDRAWAL FROM THE ACADEMIC WORLD SOME TWENTY YEARS AGO.

NOW I SUSPECTED WHERE HE HAD GONE.

FOR THE MAN I HAD STOPPED ON THE STREETS OF MIROCAW...THE MAN WITH THE DISCONCERTINGLY LETHARGIC GAZE...

...HAD VERY MUCH RESEMBLED A SUPERANNUATED VERSION OF DR. RAYMOND THOSS.

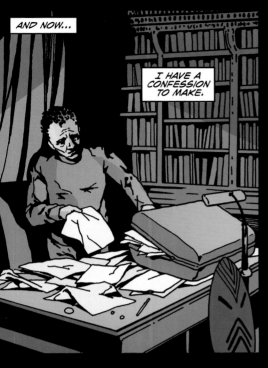

AND NOW...

I HAVE A CONFESSION TO MAKE.

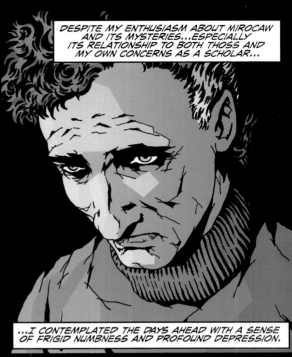

DESPITE MY ENTHUSIASM ABOUT MIROCAW AND ITS MYSTERIES...ESPECIALLY ITS RELATIONSHIP TO BOTH THOSS AND MY OWN CONCERNS AS A SCHOLAR...

...I CONTEMPLATED THE DAYS AHEAD WITH A SENSE OF FRIGID NUMBNESS AND PROFOUND DEPRESSION.

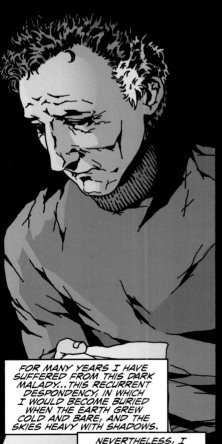

FOR MANY YEARS I HAVE SUFFERED FROM THIS DARK MALADY...THIS RECURRENT DESPONDENCY, IN WHICH I WOULD BECOME BURIED WHEN THE EARTH GREW COLD AND BARE, AND THE SKIES HEAVY WITH SHADOWS.

NEVERTHELESS, I PURSUED MY PLANS TO VISIT MIROCAW DURING ITS FESTIVAL DAYS.

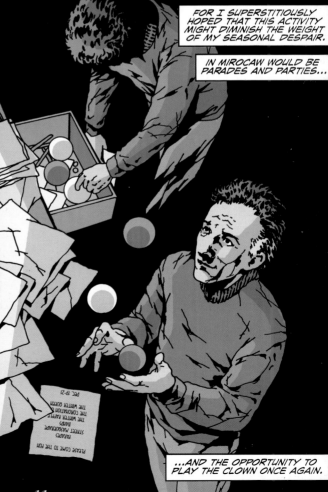

FOR I SUPERSTITIOUSLY HOPED THAT THIS ACTIVITY MIGHT DIMINISH THE WEIGHT OF MY SEASONAL DESPAIR.

IN MIROCAW WOULD BE PARADES AND PARTIES...

...AND THE OPPORTUNITY TO PLAY THE CLOWN ONCE AGAIN.

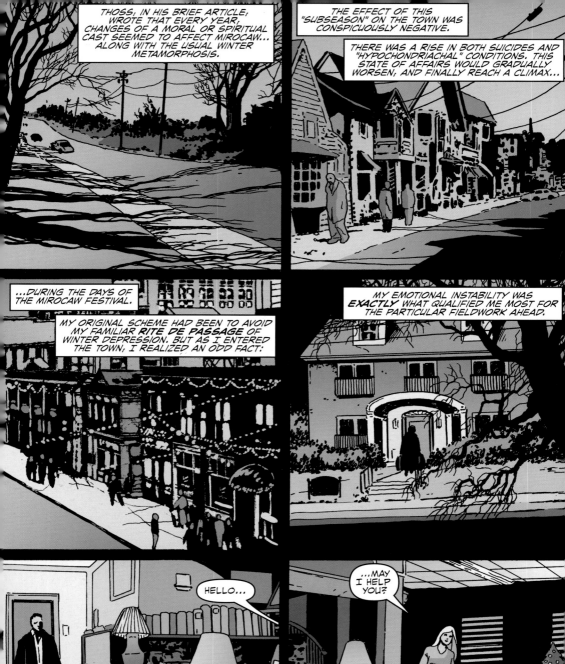

THOSS, IN HIS BRIEF ARTICLE, WROTE THAT EVERY YEAR, CHANGES OF A MORAL OR SPIRITUAL CAST SEEMED TO AFFECT MIROCAW... ALONG WITH THE USUAL WINTER METAMORPHOSIS.

THE EFFECT OF THIS "SUBSEASON" ON THE TOWN WAS CONSPICUOUSLY NEGATIVE.

THERE WAS A RISE IN BOTH SUICIDES AND "HYPOCHONDRIACHAL" CONDITIONS. THIS STATE OF AFFAIRS WOULD GRADUALLY WORSEN, AND FINALLY REACH A CLIMAX...

...DURING THE DAYS OF THE MIROCAW FESTIVAL.

MY ORIGINAL SCHEME HAD BEEN TO AVOID MY FAMILIAR *RITE DE PASSAGE* OF WINTER DEPRESSION. BUT AS I ENTERED THE TOWN, I REALIZED AN ODD FACT:

MY EMOTIONAL INSTABILITY WAS *EXACTLY* WHAT QUALIFIED ME MOST FOR THE PARTICULAR FIELDWORK AHEAD.

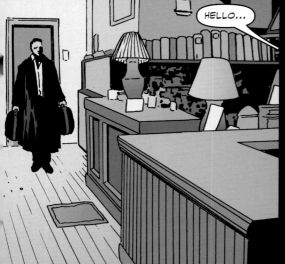

HELLO...

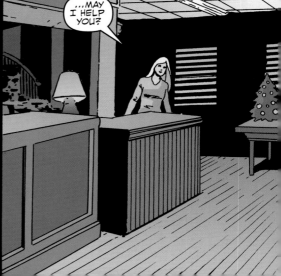

...MAY I HELP YOU?

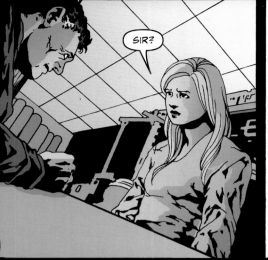
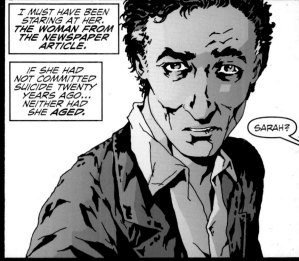

SIR?

I MUST HAVE BEEN STARING AT HER. *THE WOMAN FROM THE NEWSPAPER ARTICLE.*

IF SHE HAD NOT COMMITTED SUICIDE TWENTY YEARS AGO... NEITHER HAD SHE *AGED.*

SARAH?

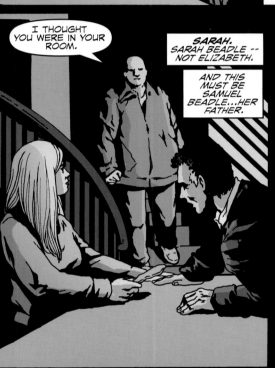
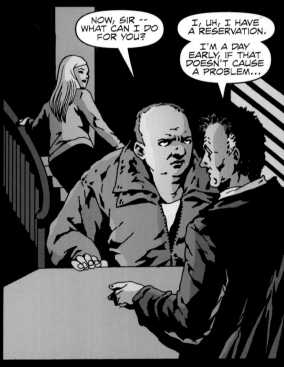

I THOUGHT YOU WERE IN YOUR ROOM.

SARAH. SARAH BEADLE -- NOT ELIZABETH.

AND THIS MUST BE SAMUEL BEADLE...HER FATHER.

NOW, SIR -- WHAT CAN I DO FOR YOU?

I, UH, I HAVE A RESERVATION.

I'M A DAY EARLY, IF THAT DOESN'T CAUSE A PROBLEM...

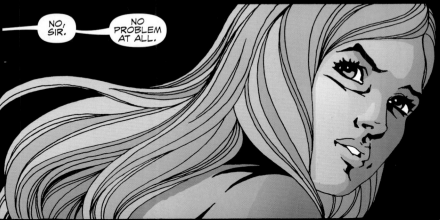

NO, SIR.

NO PROBLEM AT ALL.

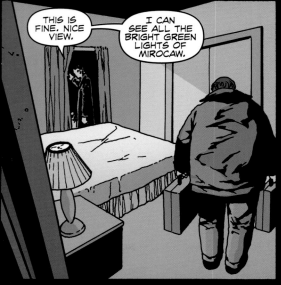

THIS IS FINE. NICE VIEW.

I CAN SEE ALL THE BRIGHT GREEN LIGHTS OF MIROCAW.

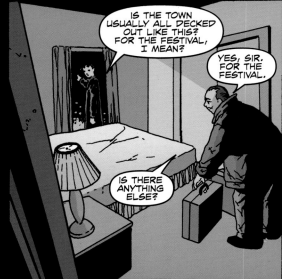

IS THE TOWN USUALLY ALL DECKED OUT LIKE THIS? FOR THE FESTIVAL, I MEAN?

YES, SIR. FOR THE FESTIVAL.

IS THERE ANYTHING ELSE?

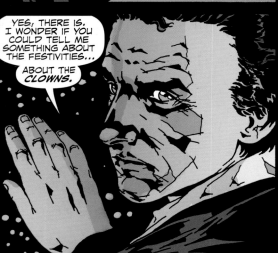

YES, THERE IS. I WONDER IF YOU COULD TELL ME SOMETHING ABOUT THE FESTIVITIES...

ABOUT THE *CLOWNS*.

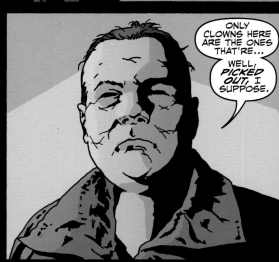

ONLY CLOWNS HERE ARE THE ONES THAT'RE...

WELL, *PICKED OUT*, I SUPPOSE.

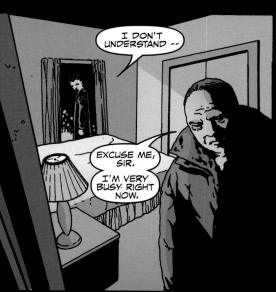

I DON'T UNDERSTAND --

EXCUSE ME, SIR. I'M VERY BUSY RIGHT NOW.

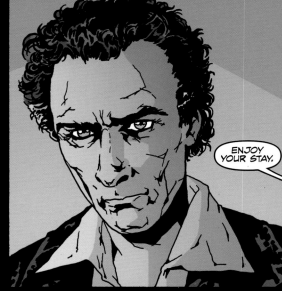

ENJOY YOUR STAY.

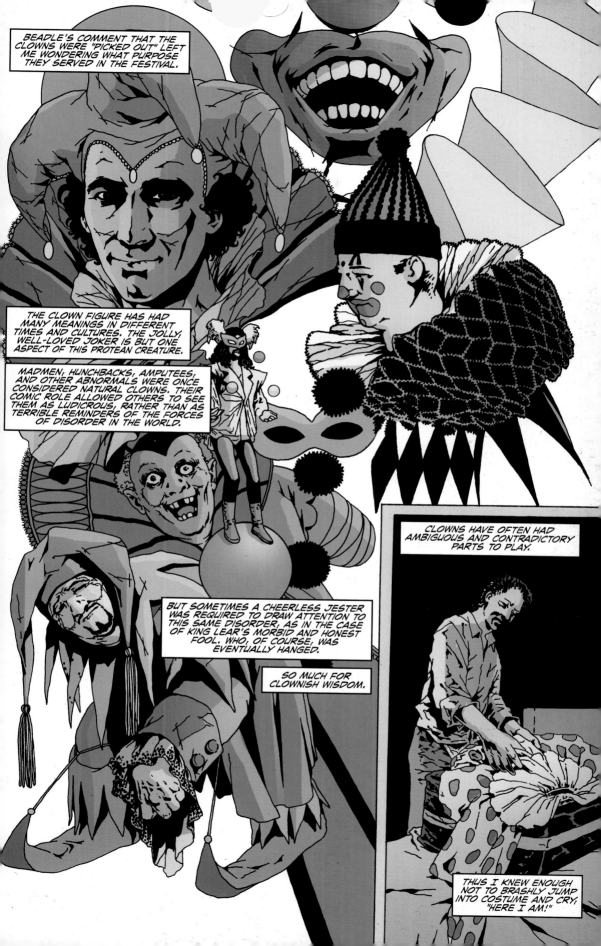

BEADLE'S COMMENT THAT THE CLOWNS WERE "PICKED OUT" LEFT ME WONDERING WHAT PURPOSE THEY SERVED IN THE FESTIVAL.

THE CLOWN FIGURE HAS HAD MANY MEANINGS IN DIFFERENT TIMES AND CULTURES. THE JOLLY, WELL-LOVED JOKER IS BUT ONE ASPECT OF THIS PROTEAN CREATURE.

MADMEN, HUNCHBACKS, AMPUTEES, AND OTHER ABNORMALS WERE ONCE CONSIDERED NATURAL CLOWNS. THEIR COMIC ROLE ALLOWED OTHERS TO SEE THEM AS LUDICROUS, RATHER THAN AS TERRIBLE REMINDERS OF THE FORCES OF DISORDER IN THE WORLD.

CLOWNS HAVE OFTEN HAD AMBIGUOUS AND CONTRADICTORY PARTS TO PLAY.

BUT SOMETIMES A CHEERLESS JESTER WAS REQUIRED TO DRAW ATTENTION TO THIS SAME DISORDER, AS IN THE CASE OF KING LEAR'S MORBID AND HONEST FOOL, WHO, OF COURSE, WAS EVENTUALLY HANGED.

SO MUCH FOR CLOWNISH WISDOM.

THUS I KNEW ENOUGH NOT TO BRASHLY JUMP INTO COSTUME AND CRY, "HERE I AM!"

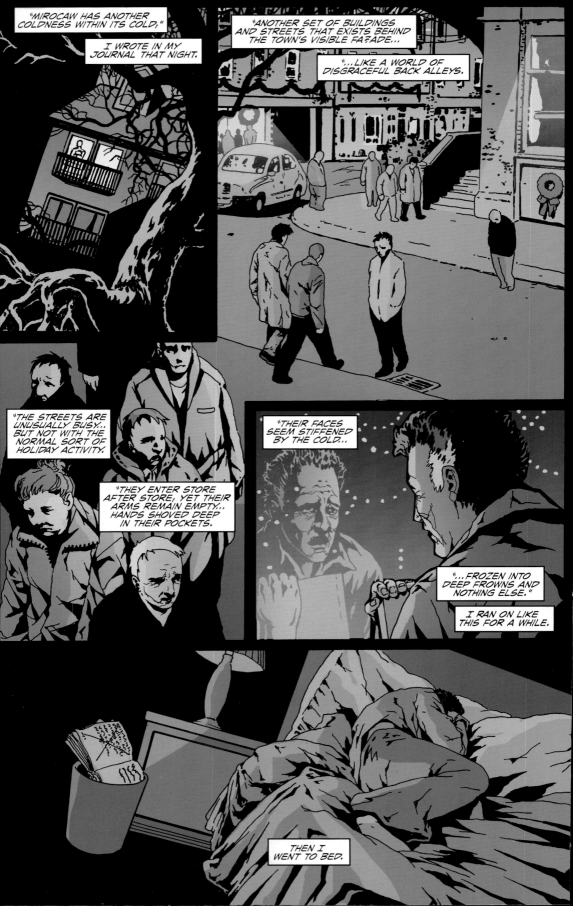

"MIROCAW HAS ANOTHER COLDNESS WITHIN ITS COLD,"

I WROTE IN MY JOURNAL THAT NIGHT.

"ANOTHER SET OF BUILDINGS AND STREETS THAT EXISTS BEHIND THE TOWN'S VISIBLE FAÇADE...

"...LIKE A WORLD OF DISGRACEFUL BACK ALLEYS.

"THE STREETS ARE UNUSUALLY BUSY... BUT NOT WITH THE NORMAL SORT OF HOLIDAY ACTIVITY.

"THEY ENTER STORE AFTER STORE, YET THEIR ARMS REMAIN EMPTY... HANDS SHOVED DEEP IN THEIR POCKETS.

"THEIR FACES SEEM STIFFENED BY THE COLD...

"...FROZEN INTO DEEP FROWNS AND NOTHING ELSE."

I RAN ON LIKE THIS FOR A WHILE.

THEN I WENT TO BED.

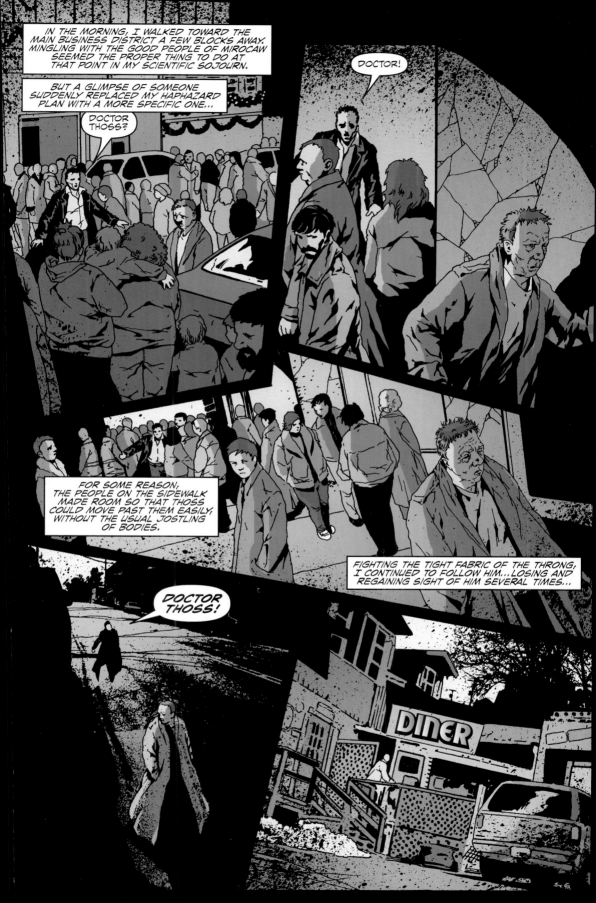

IN THE MORNING, I WALKED TOWARD THE MAIN BUSINESS DISTRICT A FEW BLOCKS AWAY. MINGLING WITH THE GOOD PEOPLE OF MIROCAW SEEMED THE PROPER THING TO DO AT THAT POINT IN MY SCIENTIFIC SOJOURN.

BUT A GLIMPSE OF SOMEONE SUDDENLY REPLACED MY HAPHAZARD PLAN WITH A MORE SPECIFIC ONE...

DOCTOR THOSS?

DOCTOR!

FOR SOME REASON, THE PEOPLE ON THE SIDEWALK MADE ROOM SO THAT THOSS COULD MOVE PAST THEM EASILY, WITHOUT THE USUAL JOSTLING OF BODIES.

FIGHTING THE TIGHT FABRIC OF THE THRONG, I CONTINUED TO FOLLOW HIM...LOSING AND REGAINING SIGHT OF HIM SEVERAL TIMES...

DOCTOR THOSS!

DINER

DOCTOR TH --
I'M -- I'M SORRY.
I THOUGHT I SAW SOMEONE I KNEW...
...COME IN HERE...

THEY SLID SLOWLY TOWARD ME IN A WORM-LIKE MASS, FILLING THE ROOM.
I WAS NOT PHYSICALLY FRIGHTENED...
...BUT THERE WERE SO MANY OF THEM.
THIS SUDDEN MOVEMENT AROUSED ME FROM MY MESMERIC DAZE.
IN A SURGE OF PANIC, I PUSHED THROUGH THEIR SOFT RANKS...
THEIR EYES SEEMED EMPTY.. UNFOCUSED. UNSEEN LEGS BECAME TANGLED WITH MY OWN; I STAGGERED AND THEN REGAINED MY BALANCE.
...AND WAS OUTSIDE.

THAT NIGHT...
SEE THE FREAK!
UUH!
SEE THE FREAK FALL.
HAHAHA!
THIS IS A DISGRACE --
WAIT! WHAT ARE YOU DOING?
CRAWL AWAY, *FREAK!*
WHO -- WHO ARE THEY? THE CLOWNS?
THEM? THEY'RE THE FREAKS.
IT'S THEIR TURN THIS YEAR. EVERYONE TAKES THEIR TURN.
NEXT YEAR IT MIGHT BE MINE. OR *YOURS.*
HA!
YOU THINK SO?

I BOUGHT THEM EACH A DRINK, AND LEARNED THAT ONLY THE OCCASIONAL GROUP OF ROWDIES ACTUALLY ENGAGED IN THE PLAYFUL ABUSE I'D SEEN. THE MAJORITY OF THE CITIZENS WERE CONTENT TO STAY ON THE SIDELINES.

I ALSO LEARNED THAT INDIVIDUALS WHO PLAYED THE CLOWNS REMAINED -- OR AT LEAST ATTEMPTED TO REMAIN -- ANONYMOUS.

WHEN, LATER, I SAW ANOTHER OF THE MIROCAW CLOWNS...

...I IMMEDIATELY THOUGHT OF THOSE INHABITANTS OF THE GHETTO DOWN THE HILL.

PERHAPS IF I HAD NOT BEEN DRINKING, I WOULD NOT HAVE TAKEN THE ACTION I DID...

WHOOPS!

THEN I REALIZED I HAD VIOLATED SOME TACIT RULE OF BEHAVIOR... THOUGH I HAD THOUGHT MY ACTION WELL WITHIN THE COMMON PRACTICE.

THE IDEA OCCURRED TO ME THAT I MIGHT EVEN BE APPREHENDED AND PROSECUTED FOR WHAT, IN ANY OTHER CIRCUMSTANCES, WAS CERTAINLY A CRIMINAL ACT.

I TURNED TO HELP THE CLOWN BACK TO HIS FEET, HOPING TO SOMEHOW REDEEM MY OFFENSE. BUT THE CREATURE WAS GONE.

SO I WALKED AWAY, SOLEMNLY, FROM THE SCENE OF MY INADVERTENT CRIME.

HAHAHA!

SEE THE FREAK --

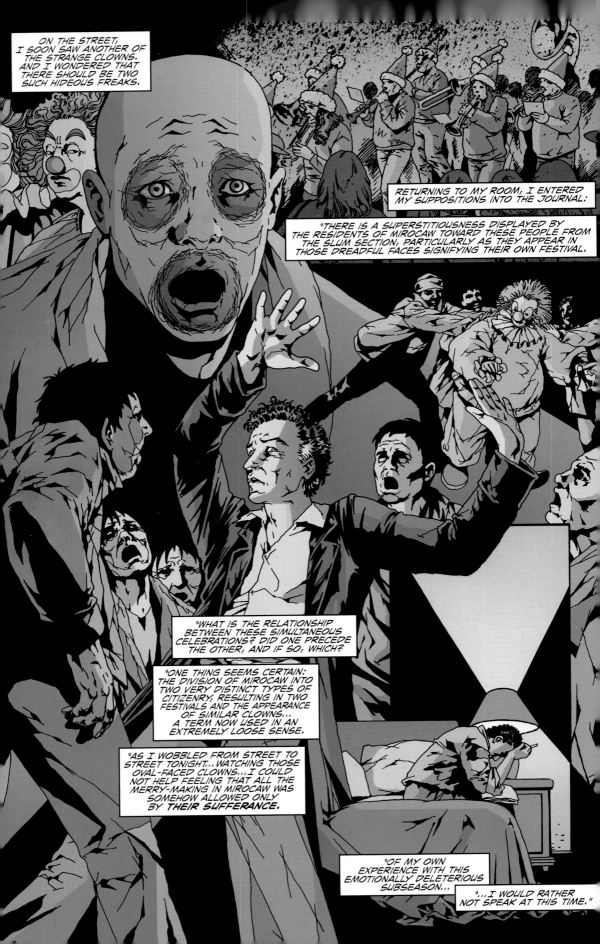

ON THE STREET, I SOON SAW ANOTHER OF THE STRANGE CLOWNS. AND I WONDERED THAT THERE SHOULD BE TWO SUCH HIDEOUS FREAKS.

RETURNING TO MY ROOM, I ENTERED MY SUPPOSITIONS INTO THE JOURNAL:

"THERE IS A SUPERSTITIOUSNESS DISPLAYED BY THE RESIDENTS OF MIROCAW TOWARD THESE PEOPLE FROM THE SLUM SECTION, PARTICULARLY AS THEY APPEAR IN THOSE DREADFUL FACES SIGNIFYING THEIR OWN FESTIVAL.

"WHAT IS THE RELATIONSHIP BETWEEN THESE SIMULTANEOUS CELEBRATIONS? DID ONE PRECEDE THE OTHER, AND IF SO, WHICH?

"ONE THING SEEMS CERTAIN: THE DIVISION OF MIROCAW INTO TWO VERY DISTINCT TYPES OF CITIZENRY, RESULTING IN TWO FESTIVALS AND THE APPEARANCE OF SIMILAR CLOWNS... A TERM NOW USED IN AN EXTREMELY LOOSE SENSE.

"AS I WOBBLED FROM STREET TO STREET TONIGHT... WATCHING THOSE OVAL-FACED CLOWNS... I COULD NOT HELP FEELING THAT ALL THE MERRY-MAKING IN MIROCAW WAS SOMEHOW ALLOWED ONLY BY THEIR SUFFERANCE.

"OF MY OWN EXPERIENCE WITH THIS EMOTIONALLY DELETERIOUS SUBSEASON...

"...I WOULD RATHER NOT SPEAK AT THIS TIME."

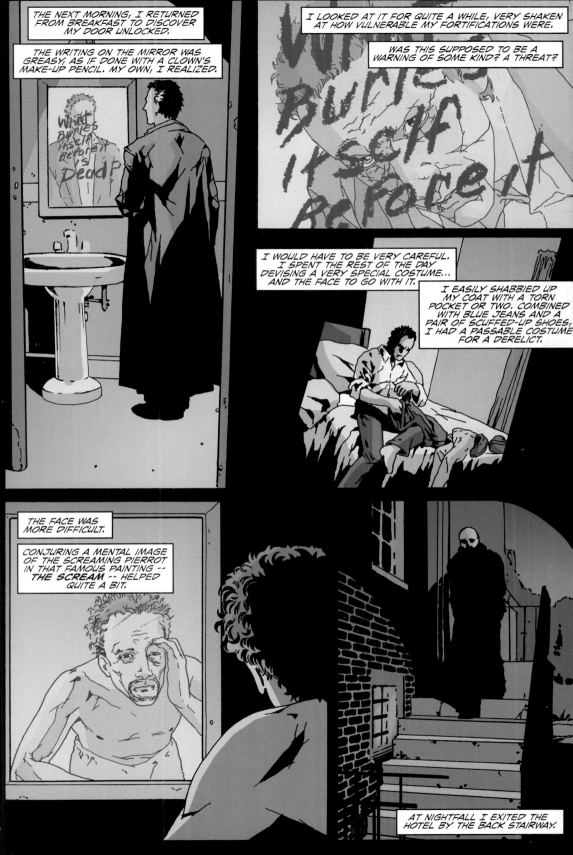

THE NEXT MORNING, I RETURNED FROM BREAKFAST TO DISCOVER MY DOOR UNLOCKED.

THE WRITING ON THE MIRROR WAS GREASY, AS IF DONE WITH A CLOWN'S MAKE-UP PENCIL. MY OWN, I REALIZED.

I LOOKED AT IT FOR QUITE A WHILE, VERY SHAKEN AT HOW VULNERABLE MY FORTIFICATIONS WERE.

WAS THIS SUPPOSED TO BE A WARNING OF SOME KIND? A THREAT?

I WOULD HAVE TO BE VERY CAREFUL. I SPENT THE REST OF THE DAY DEVISING A VERY SPECIAL COSTUME... AND THE FACE TO GO WITH IT.

I EASILY SHABBIED UP MY COAT WITH A TORN POCKET OR TWO. COMBINED WITH BLUE JEANS AND A PAIR OF SCUFFED-UP SHOES, I HAD A PASSABLE COSTUME FOR A DERELICT.

THE FACE WAS MORE DIFFICULT.

CONJURING A MENTAL IMAGE OF THE SCREAMING PIERROT IN THAT FAMOUS PAINTING -- THE SCREAM -- HELPED QUITE A BIT.

AT NIGHTFALL I EXITED THE HOTEL BY THE BACK STAIRWAY.

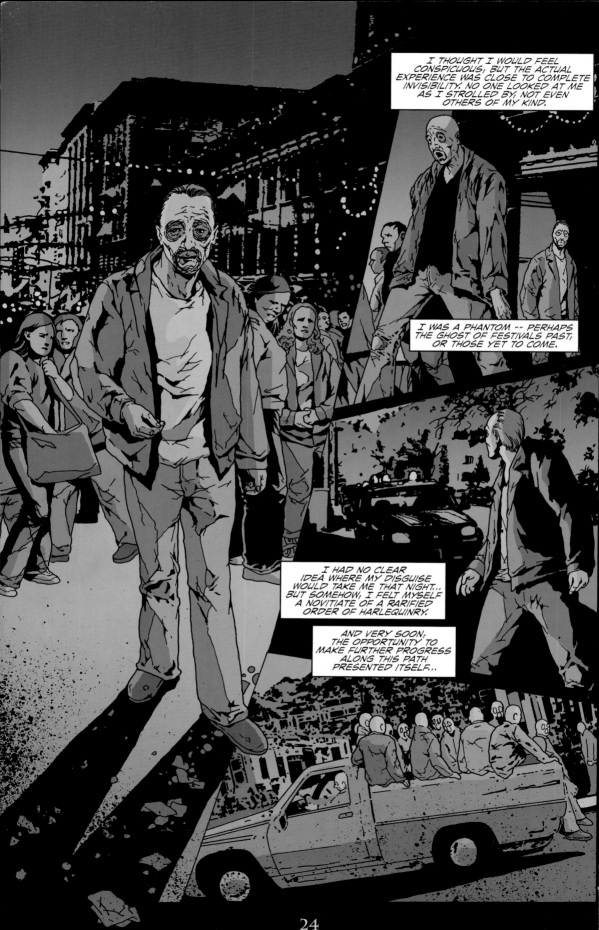

I THOUGHT I WOULD FEEL CONSPICUOUS, BUT THE ACTUAL EXPERIENCE WAS CLOSE TO COMPLETE INVISIBILITY. NO ONE LOOKED AT ME AS I STROLLED BY. NOT EVEN OTHERS OF MY KIND.

I WAS A PHANTOM -- PERHAPS THE GHOST OF FESTIVALS PAST, OR THOSE YET TO COME.

I HAD NO CLEAR IDEA WHERE MY DISGUISE WOULD TAKE ME THAT NIGHT... BUT SOMEHOW, I FELT MYSELF A NOVITIATE OF A RARIFIED ORDER OF HARLEQUINRY.

AND VERY SOON, THE OPPORTUNITY TO MAKE FURTHER PROGRESS ALONG THIS PATH PRESENTED ITSELF...

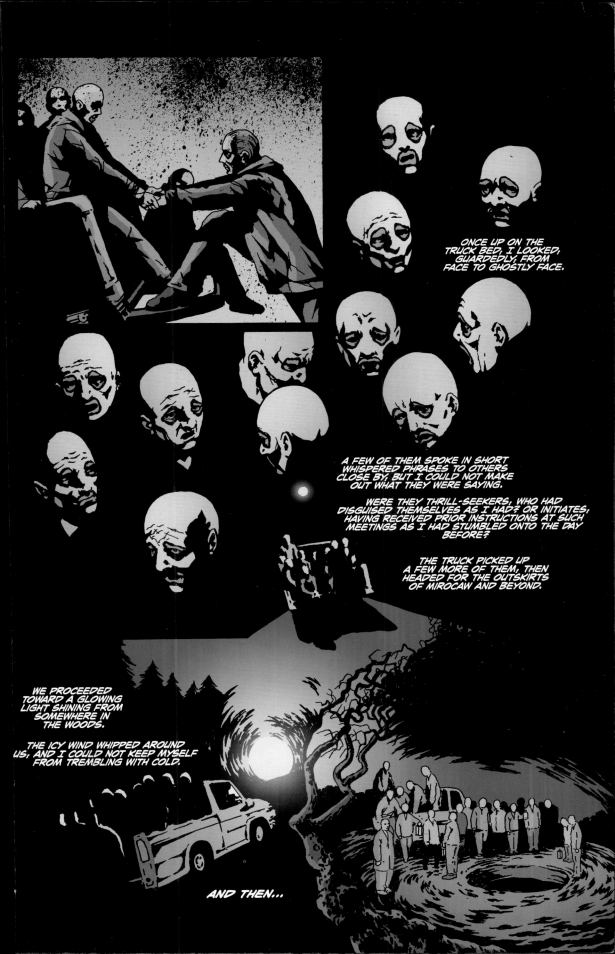

ONCE UP ON THE
TRUCK BED, I LOOKED,
GUARDEDLY, FROM
FACE TO GHOSTLY FACE.

A FEW OF THEM SPOKE IN SHORT
WHISPERED PHRASES TO OTHERS
CLOSE BY, BUT I COULD NOT MAKE
OUT WHAT THEY WERE SAYING.

WERE THEY THRILL-SEEKERS, WHO HAD
DISGUISED THEMSELVES AS I HAD? OR INITIATES,
HAVING RECEIVED PRIOR INSTRUCTIONS AT SUCH
MEETINGS AS I HAD STUMBLED ONTO THE DAY
BEFORE?

THE TRUCK PICKED UP
A FEW MORE OF THEM, THEN
HEADED FOR THE OUTSKIRTS
OF MIROCAW AND BEYOND.

WE PROCEEDED
TOWARD A GLOWING
LIGHT SHINING FROM
SOMEWHERE IN
THE WOODS.

THE ICY WIND WHIPPED AROUND
US, AND I COULD NOT KEEP MYSELF
FROM TREMBLING WITH COLD.

AND THEN...

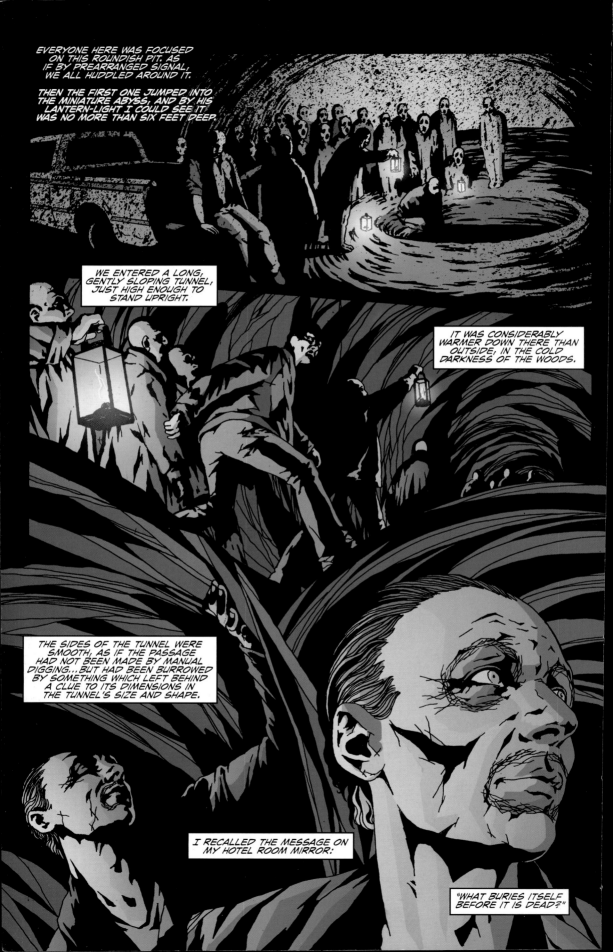

EVERYONE HERE WAS FOCUSED ON THIS ROUNDISH PIT. AS IF BY PREARRANGED SIGNAL, WE ALL HUDDLED AROUND IT.

THEN THE FIRST ONE JUMPED INTO THE MINIATURE ABYSS, AND BY HIS LANTERN-LIGHT I COULD SEE IT WAS NO MORE THAN SIX FEET DEEP.

WE ENTERED A LONG, GENTLY SLOPING TUNNEL, JUST HIGH ENOUGH TO STAND UPRIGHT.

IT WAS CONSIDERABLY WARMER DOWN THERE THAN OUTSIDE, IN THE COLD DARKNESS OF THE WOODS.

THE SIDES OF THE TUNNEL WERE SMOOTH, AS IF THE PASSAGE HAD NOT BEEN MADE BY MANUAL DIGGING...BUT HAD BEEN BURROWED BY SOMETHING WHICH LEFT BEHIND A CLUE TO ITS DIMENSIONS IN THE TUNNEL'S SIZE AND SHAPE.

I RECALLED THE MESSAGE ON MY HOTEL ROOM MIRROR:

"WHAT BURIES ITSELF BEFORE IT IS DEAD?"

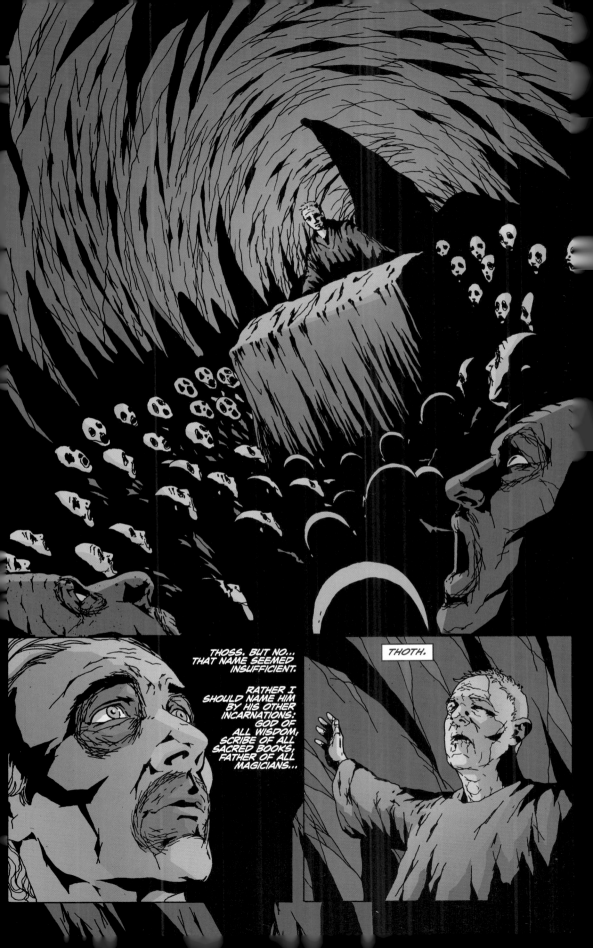

THOSS. BUT NO...
THAT NAME SEEMED
INSUFFICIENT.

RATHER I
SHOULD NAME HIM
BY HIS OTHER
INCARNATIONS:
GOD OF
ALL WISDOM,
SCRIBE OF ALL
SACRED BOOKS;
FATHER OF ALL
MAGICIANS...

THOTH.

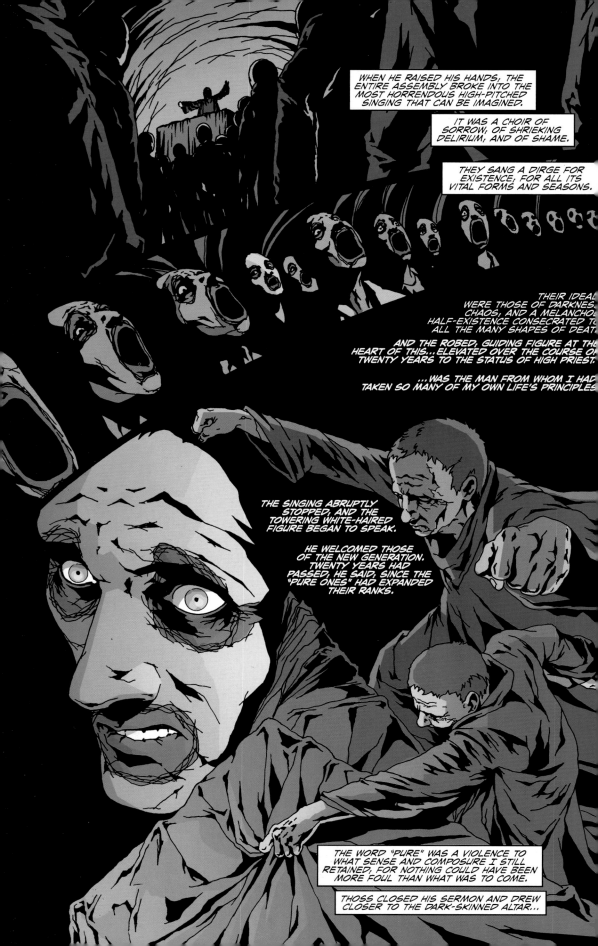

WHEN HE RAISED HIS HANDS, THE ENTIRE ASSEMBLY BROKE INTO THE MOST HORRENDOUS HIGH-PITCHED SINGING THAT CAN BE IMAGINED.

IT WAS A CHOIR OF SORROW, OF SHRIEKING DELIRIUM, AND OF SHAME.

THEY SANG A DIRGE FOR EXISTENCE, FOR ALL ITS VITAL FORMS AND SEASONS.

THEIR IDEAL WERE THOSE OF DARKNES, CHAOS, AND A MELANCHO HALF-EXISTENCE CONSECRATED T ALL THE MANY SHAPES OF DEAT

AND THE ROBED, GUIDING FIGURE AT THE HEART OF THIS...ELEVATED OVER THE COURSE O TWENTY YEARS TO THE STATUS OF HIGH PRIEST.

...WAS THE MAN FROM WHOM I HAD TAKEN SO MANY OF MY OWN LIFE'S PRINCIPLES

THE SINGING ABRUPTLY STOPPED, AND THE TOWERING WHITE-HAIRED FIGURE BEGAN TO SPEAK.

HE WELCOMED THOSE OF THE NEW GENERATION. TWENTY YEARS HAD PASSED, HE SAID, SINCE THE "PURE ONES" HAD EXPANDED THEIR RANKS.

THE WORD "PURE" WAS A VIOLENCE TO WHAT SENSE AND COMPOSURE I STILL RETAINED; FOR NOTHING COULD HAVE BEEN MORE FOUL THAN WHAT WAS TO COME.

THOSS CLOSED HIS SERMON AND DREW CLOSER TO THE DARK-SKINNED ALTAR...

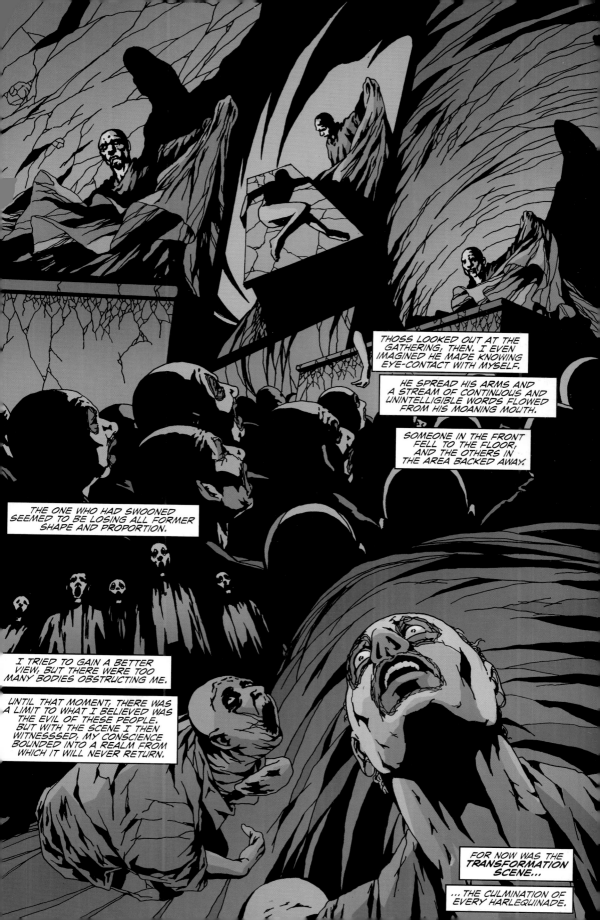

THOSS LOOKED OUT AT THE GATHERING, THEN. I EVEN IMAGINED HE MADE KNOWING EYE-CONTACT WITH MYSELF.

HE SPREAD HIS ARMS AND A STREAM OF CONTINUOUS AND UNINTELLIGIBLE WORDS FLOWED FROM HIS MOANING MOUTH.

SOMEONE IN THE FRONT FELL TO THE FLOOR, AND THE OTHERS IN THE AREA BACKED AWAY.

THE ONE WHO HAD SWOONED SEEMED TO BE LOSING ALL FORMER SHAPE AND PROPORTION.

I TRIED TO GAIN A BETTER VIEW, BUT THERE WERE TOO MANY BODIES OBSTRUCTING ME.

UNTIL THAT MOMENT, THERE WAS A LIMIT TO WHAT I BELIEVED WAS THE EVIL OF THESE PEOPLE. BUT WITH THE SCENE I THEN WITNESSSED, MY CONSCIENCE BOUNDED INTO A REALM FROM WHICH IT WILL NEVER RETURN.

FOR NOW WAS THE TRANSFORMATION SCENE...

...THE CULMINATION OF EVERY HARLEQUINADE.

AT FIRST I THOUGHT IT WAS A CLOWN'S TRICK.
O GOD, HARLEQUIN, DO NOT MOVE LIKE THAT!
HARLEQUIN, WHERE ARE YOUR ARMS?
AND YOUR LEGS HAVE MELTED TOGETHER AND BEGUN SQUIRMING UPON THE FLOOR!
THE TRANSFORMATION OF HARLEQUIN, THROWING OFF HIS FOOL'S FACADE.
WHAT HORRIBLE, MOUTHING UMBILICUS IS THAT WHERE YOUR FACE SHOULD BE?
WHAT IS IT THAT BURIES ITSELF BEFORE IT IS DEAD?
THE ALMIGHTY SERPENT OF WISDOM.
THE CONQUEROR WORM.

AAAAAA--!!

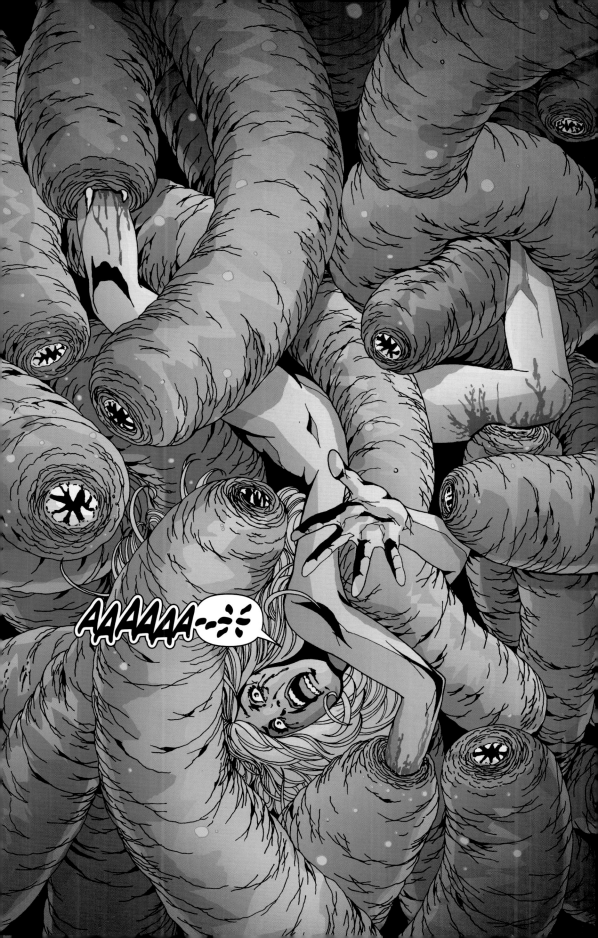

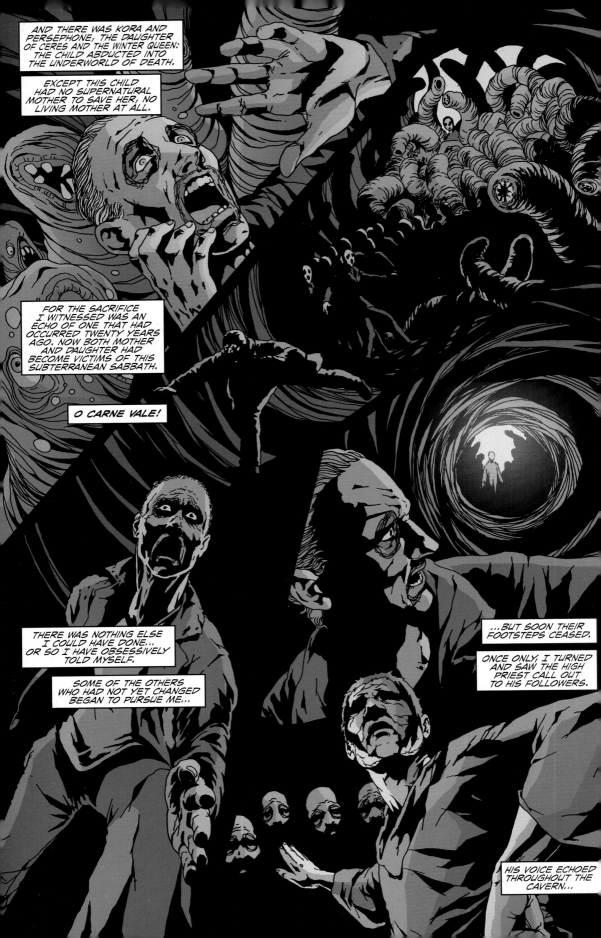

AND THERE WAS KORA AND PERSEPHONE, THE DAUGHTER OF CERES AND THE WINTER QUEEN: THE CHILD ABDUCTED INTO THE UNDERWORLD OF DEATH.

EXCEPT THIS CHILD HAD NO SUPERNATURAL MOTHER TO SAVE HER, NO LIVING MOTHER AT ALL.

FOR THE SACRIFICE I WITNESSED WAS AN ECHO OF ONE THAT HAD OCCURRED TWENTY YEARS AGO. NOW BOTH MOTHER AND DAUGHTER HAD BECOME VICTIMS OF THIS SUBTERRANEAN SABBATH.

O CARNE VALE!

THERE WAS NOTHING ELSE I COULD HAVE DONE... OR SO I HAVE OBSESSIVELY TOLD MYSELF.

SOME OF THE OTHERS WHO HAD NOT YET CHANGED BEGAN TO PURSUE ME...

...BUT SOON THEIR FOOTSTEPS CEASED.

ONCE ONLY, I TURNED AND SAW THE HIGH PRIEST CALL OUT TO HIS FOLLOWERS.

HIS VOICE ECHOED THROUGHOUT THE CAVERN...

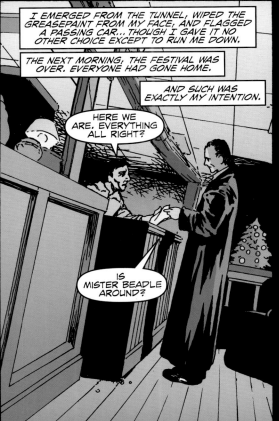

I EMERGED FROM THE TUNNEL, WIPED THE GREASEPAINT FROM MY FACE, AND FLAGGED A PASSING CAR...THOUGH I GAVE IT NO OTHER CHOICE EXCEPT TO RUN ME DOWN.

THE NEXT MORNING, THE FESTIVAL WAS OVER. EVERYONE HAD GONE HOME.

AND SUCH WAS EXACTLY MY INTENTION.

HERE WE ARE. EVERYTHING ALL RIGHT?

IS MISTER BEADLE AROUND?

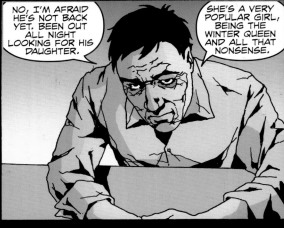

NO, I'M AFRAID HE'S NOT BACK YET. BEEN OUT ALL NIGHT LOOKING FOR HIS DAUGHTER.

SHE'S A VERY POPULAR GIRL, BEING THE WINTER QUEEN AND ALL THAT NONSENSE.

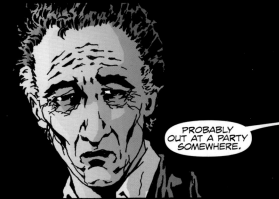

PROBABLY OUT AT A PARTY SOMEWHERE.

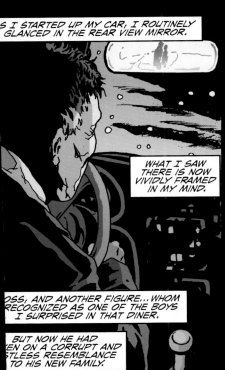

S I STARTED UP MY CAR, I ROUTINELY GLANCED IN THE REAR VIEW MIRROR.

WHAT I SAW THERE IS NOW VIVIDLY FRAMED IN MY MIND.

OSS, AND ANOTHER FIGURE...WHOM RECOGNIZED AS ONE OF THE BOYS I SURPRISED IN THAT DINER.

BUT NOW HE HAD EN ON A CORRUPT AND STLESS RESEMBLANCE TO HIS NEW FAMILY.

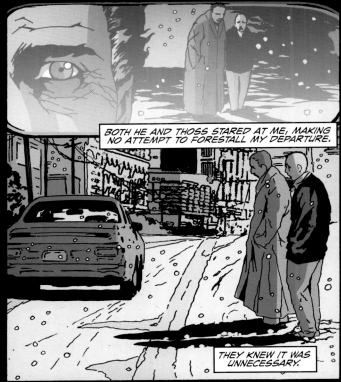

BOTH HE AND THOSS STARED AT ME, MAKING NO ATTEMPT TO FORESTALL MY DEPARTURE.

THEY KNEW IT WAS UNNECESSARY.

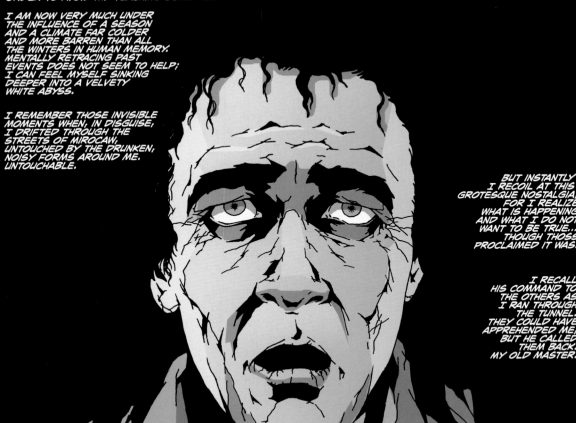

ONLY NOW HAS THE FULL WEIGHT OF MY EXPERIENCE DESCENDED UPON ME. SO FAR I HAVE CLAIMED ILLNESS IN ORDER TO AVOID MY TEACHING SCHEDULE.

I AM NOW VERY MUCH UNDER THE INFLUENCE OF A SEASON AND A CLIMATE FAR COLDER AND MORE BARREN THAN ALL THE WINTERS IN HUMAN MEMORY. MENTALLY RETRACING PAST EVENTS DOES NOT SEEM TO HELP; I CAN FEEL MYSELF SINKING DEEPER INTO A VELVETY WHITE ABYSS.

I REMEMBER THOSE INVISIBLE MOMENTS WHEN, IN DISGUISE, I DRIFTED THROUGH THE STREETS OF MIROCAW, UNTOUCHED BY THE DRUNKEN, NOISY FORMS AROUND ME. UNTOUCHABLE.

BUT INSTANTLY I RECOIL AT THIS GROTESQUE NOSTALGIA, FOR I REALIZE WHAT IS HAPPENING AND WHAT I DO NOT WANT TO BE TRUE... THOUGH THOSS PROCLAIMED IT WAS.

I RECALL HIS COMMAND TO THE OTHERS AS I RAN THROUGH THE TUNNEL. THEY COULD HAVE APPREHENDED ME, BUT HE CALLED THEM BACK. MY OLD MASTER.

HIS VOICE ECHOED THROUGHOUT THAT CAVERN, AND NOW IT REVERBERATES WITHIN MY OWN PSYCHIC CHAMBERS OF MEMORY.

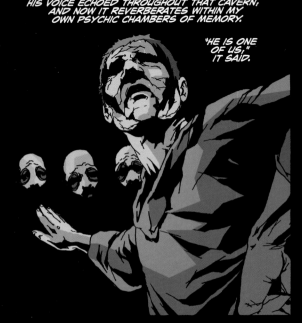

"HE IS ONE OF US," IT SAID.

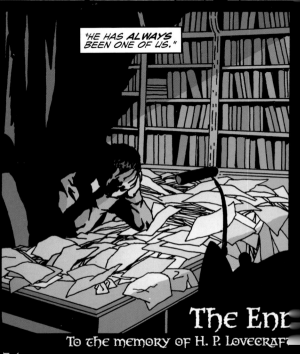

"HE HAS ALWAYS BEEN ONE OF US."

The End

To the memory of H. P. Lovecraft

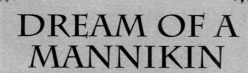

DREAM OF A MANNIKIN

Dolls, mannikins, puppets, marionettes, and other little effigies of us: how often they seem to pop up in horror narratives. For the most part, they are just bit players in what Robert Louis Stevenson called "bogey tales." They are extras who turn up in order to lend their spooky presence for the sake of atmosphere alone, while the true menace of the narrative is something else altogether.

Most typically, in fact, dolls, mannikins, puppets, and marionettes are props lying about in a bogey tale, frozen faces seen in the moonlight shining into a child's bedroom, dismembered arms and legs, or decapitated plastic heads that once graced a department store display window and since have been relegated to spare parts strewn about an old warehouse where such things are stored or sent to die. In this capacity they have a nice symbolic value, as they seem connected to another world, one that is all harm and disorder—the kind of place we sometimes fear is the model for our own home ground, which we believe is basically sound and secure, or at least one in which we do not mistake a counterfeit person for the real thing. This is what happens to the protagonist of E. T. A. Hoffmann's *The Sandman* just before he screams, "Turn and turn about, little doll!" and throws himself to his death from a tower. After this tragedy, goes Hoffman's story, "Many lovers, to be quite convinced that they were not enamored of wooden dolls, would request their mistresses to sing and dance a little out of time, to embroider and knit, and play with their lapdogs, while listening to reading, etc., and, above all, not merely to listen, but also sometimes to talk, in such a manner as presupposed actual thought and feeling." The lesson: none of us can really be sure of what we are or may become.

There are many awful fates in horror stories, and among the worst of them is when a human form becomes objectified as a doll, a mannikin, a puppet, or a marionette. This is the point in which a character actually enters a world that he thought was just a creepy little place inside of ours. How unpleasant to find that this plane of existence, which we thought was at worst a symbol of the sinister, is actually a sphere that looks down upon the one in which we dwell. Just as we know that dreams are merely reflections of what happens in our lives, we are also quite sure that dolls, mannikins, puppets, and marionettes are only reflections of ourselves. No juncture could exist, we believe, between dreams and life or between those little effigies of our bodies and the flesh itself. That would be too terrible a fate, for things to become confused in such a way. More terrible, of course, would be to find that this confusion is a reality—that a dream of a mannikin, or other things of a like nature, is not a dream at all.

ONCE UPON A WEDNESDAY AFTERNOON, A GIRL STEPPED INTO MY OFFICE.
IT WAS HER FIRST SESSION, AND SHE INTRODUCED HERSELF AS MISS AMY LOCHER.
"AMY."
DIDN'T YOU ONCE TELL ME THAT... LONG AGO...
...YOU HAD A DOLL BY THAT NAME?
MISS LOCHER WAS DRESSED IN MUCH THE SAME CLASSIC STYLE WHICH YOU NORMALLY FAVOR.
HER REASON FOR VISITING ME -- AS YOU MAY OR MAY NOT KNOW -- INVOLVED A DISTRESSING DREAM SHE HAD RECENTLY SUFFERED.
LIKE THOSE STATE WITNESSES THE GOVERNMENT WISHES TO PROTECT WITH NEW IDENTITIES, SHE HAS BEEN OUTFITTED BY THE DREAM WITH A REMARKABLY COMPLETE BIOGRAPHY.
A MARVELOUS TRICK OF THE MIND, THIS.

Chicago Public Library
Scottsdale
2/25/2017   2:20:01 PM
-Patron Receipt-

ITEMS BORROWED:

1:
Title: The nightmare factory : based on the
Item #: R0413190907
Due Date: 3/18/2017

2:
Title: Halloween
Item #: R0335061636
Due Date: 3/4/2017

-Please retain for your records-

LYU

IN THE DREAM, MISS LOCHER'S WORKING DAY FINDS HER AS A LONG-TIME EMPLOYEE OF A FASHIONABLE CLOTHES SHOP.

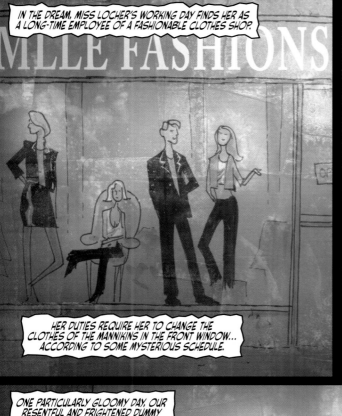

HER DUTIES REQUIRE HER TO CHANGE THE CLOTHES OF THE MANNIKINS IN THE FRONT WINDOW... ACCORDING TO SOME MYSTERIOUS SCHEDULE.

HER ENTIRE EXISTENCE IS SLAVISHLY GIVEN OVER TO DRESSING AND UNDRESSING THESE DUMMIES.

SHE IS PROFOUNDLY DISSATISFIED WITH HER LOT, AND THE MANNIKINS BECOME THE FOCAL POINT OF HER ANIMUS.

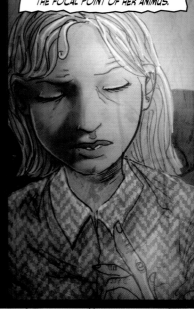

ONE PARTICULARLY GLOOMY DAY, OUR RESENTFUL AND FRIGHTENED DUMMY DRESSER APPROACHES HER WORK.

SHE BITTERLY SURVEYS THE RANKS OF THESE PUTTY-FACED CREATURES.

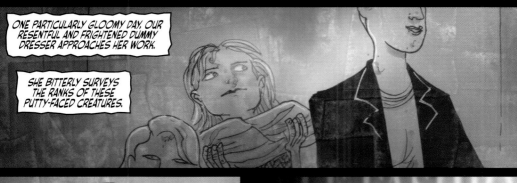

THEIR UNWARM, UNCOLD BODIES REPEL HER TOUCH.

ALMOST RITUALLY, SHE SAYS:

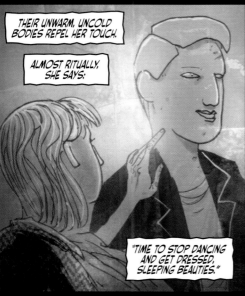

"TIME TO STOP DANCING AND GET DRESSED, SLEEPING BEAUTIES."

BUT BEFORE THE DRESSER IS ABLE TO PUT ONE STITCH ON THEM...

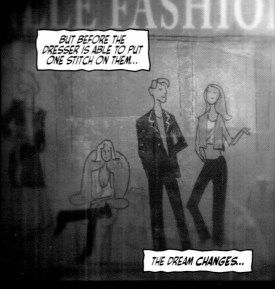

THE DREAM CHANGES...

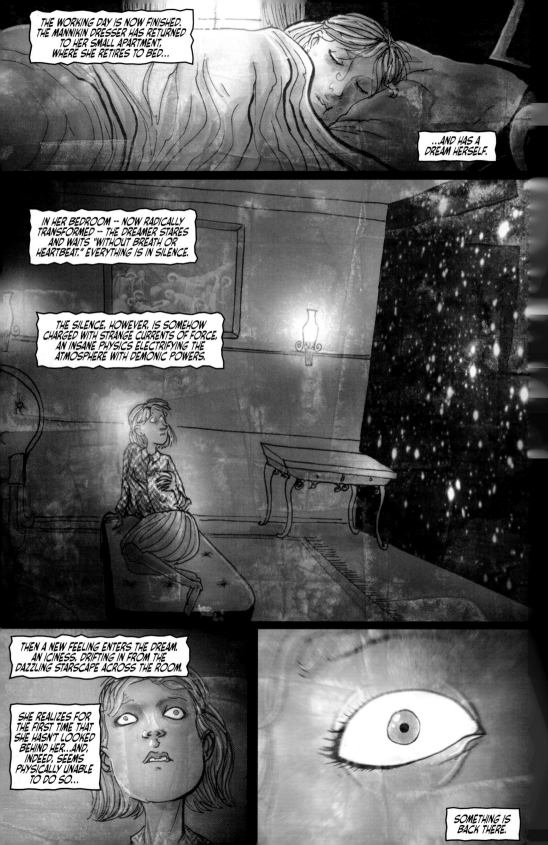

THE WORKING DAY IS NOW FINISHED. THE MANNIKIN DRESSER HAS RETURNED TO HER SMALL APARTMENT, WHERE SHE RETIRES TO BED...

...AND HAS A DREAM HERSELF.

IN HER BEDROOM -- NOW RADICALLY TRANSFORMED -- THE DREAMER STARES AND WAITS "WITHOUT BREATH OR HEARTBEAT." EVERYTHING IS IN SILENCE.

THE SILENCE, HOWEVER, IS SOMEHOW CHARGED WITH STRANGE CURRENTS OF FORCE, AN INSANE PHYSICS ELECTRIFYING THE ATMOSPHERE WITH DEMONIC POWERS.

THEN A NEW FEELING ENTERS THE DREAM. AN ICINESS, DRIFTING IN FROM THE DAZZLING STARSCAPE ACROSS THE ROOM.

SHE REALIZES FOR THE FIRST TIME THAT SHE HASN'T LOOKED BEHIND HER...AND, INDEED, SEEMS PHYSICALLY UNABLE TO DO SO...

SOMETHING IS BACK THERE.

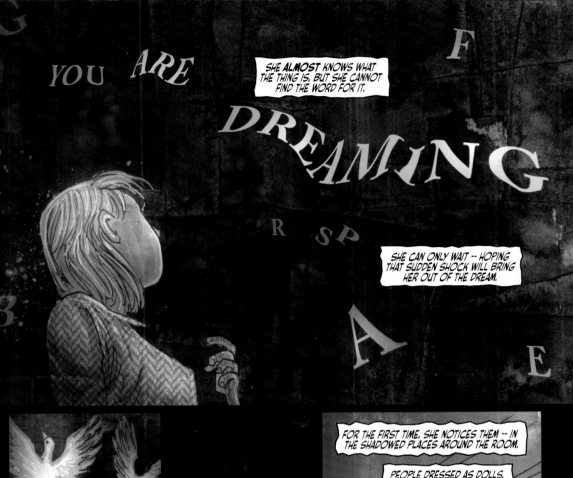

SHE **ALMOST** KNOWS WHAT THE THING IS, BUT SHE CANNOT FIND THE WORD FOR IT.

SHE CAN ONLY WAIT -- HOPING THAT SUDDEN SHOCK WILL BRING HER OUT OF THE DREAM.

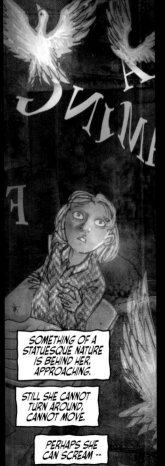

SOMETHING OF A STATUESQUE NATURE IS BEHIND HER, APPROACHING.

STILL SHE CANNOT TURN AROUND, CANNOT MOVE.

PERHAPS SHE CAN SCREAM --

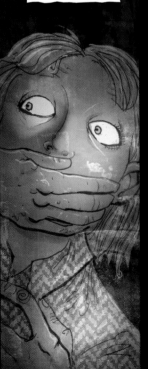

THE FINGERS ON HER LIPS FEEL LIKE THICK, NAKED CRAYONS.

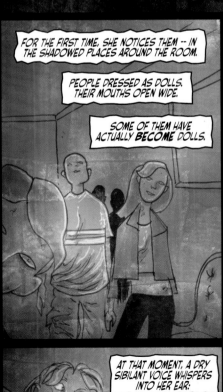

FOR THE FIRST TIME, SHE NOTICES THEM -- IN THE SHADOWED PLACES AROUND THE ROOM.

PEOPLE DRESSED AS DOLLS, THEIR MOUTHS OPEN WIDE.

SOME OF THEM HAVE ACTUALLY **BECOME** DOLLS.

AT THAT MOMENT, A DRY SIBILANT VOICE WHISPERS INTO HER EAR:

"TIME TO GET DRESSED, LITTLE DOLLING..."

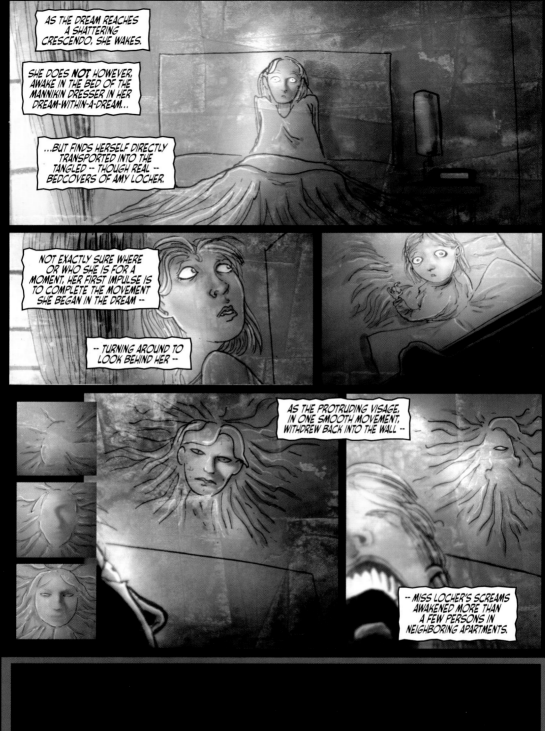

AS THE DREAM REACHES A SHATTERING CRESCENDO, SHE WAKES.

SHE DOES **NOT**, HOWEVER, AWAKE IN THE BED OF THE MANNIKIN DRESSER IN HER DREAM-WITHIN-A-DREAM...

...BUT FINDS HERSELF DIRECTLY TRANSPORTED INTO THE TANGLED -- THOUGH REAL -- BEDCOVERS OF AMY LOCHER.

NOT EXACTLY SURE WHERE OR WHO SHE IS FOR A MOMENT, HER FIRST IMPULSE IS TO COMPLETE THE MOVEMENT SHE BEGAN IN THE DREAM --

-- TURNING AROUND TO LOOK BEHIND HER --

AS THE PROTRUDING VISAGE, IN ONE SMOOTH MOVEMENT, WITHDREW BACK INTO THE WALL --

-- MISS LOCHER'S SCREAMS AWAKENED MORE THAN A FEW PERSONS IN NEIGHBORING APARTMENTS.

END OF DREAM AND RELATED EXPERIENCES.

Now my darling
...YOU CAN IMAGINE MY REACTION TO THIS PSYCHIC YARN. EVERY LOOSE SKEIN I FOLLOWED LED ME BACK TO YOU.
I REFER TO THOSE "OTHERWORLDS" YOU CLAIM YOU'VE DETECTED THROUGH A COMBINATION OF OCCULT STUDIES AND DEPTH ANALYSIS.
IT ALL REMINDS ME OF THAT TRITE LITTLE CHINESE FABLE OF THE MAN WHO DREAMED HE WAS A BUTTERFLY...THEN AFFECTED NOT TO KNOW WHETHER HE WAS A MAN WHO'D DREAMED HE WAS A BUTTERFLY OR A BUTTERFLY NOW DREAMING...
THE REAL QUESTION IS: DO BUTTERFLIES DREAM?
(ANSWER: NO. RECALL THE LAB STUDIES IN THIS FIELD, IF YOU WILL, FOR ONCE.)
END OF ISSUE.
SURELY YOU CAN SEE HOW MISS LOCHER'S IDENTITY TRICKS FIT IN WITH YOUR OWN, ARCANE STUDIES.
CONTEMPLATING HER DREAM...AND THE EXTENT OF HER DISTRESS...
...I ACTUALLY CAME TO BELIEVE IN A SOLIPSISTIC DREAM DEITY COMMANDING ALL IT SEES. ALL OF WHICH IS ACTUALLY, AND ONLY, ITSELF.
SEE WHAT YOU'VE DONE TO ME! I ALWAYS TRY TO ARGUE YOUR CASE, MY LOVE -- I CAN'T HELP MYSELF.
BUT I DON'T THINK IT'S RIGHT TO BE EXERTING YOUR INFLUENCE ON INNOCENTS...LIKE MISS LOCHER.

I SHOULD TELL YOU THAT I HYPNOTIZED THE GIRL.
SHE RECOUNTED MUCH THE SAME EVENTS AS BEFORE...WITH ONE IMPORTANT EXCEPTION.
WHEN MY PATIENT HAD FIRST DESCRIBED HER DREAM DRAMA TO ME, SHE HAD FORGOTTEN ANOTHER CHARACTER HIDDEN IN THE BACKGROUND.
THE PROPRIETOR OF THE NAMELESS CLOTHING STORE... A DOMINEERING BOSS...
...PLAYED BY A CERTAIN LADY PSYCHOANALYST.
YES, MY DEAR -- YOU WERE PRESENT IN MISS LOCHER'S HYPNOTIC STATEMENT.
I REFRAINED FROM ASKING MY NEW PATIENT ANYTHING ABOUT HER RELATIONSHIP WITH YOU...AND I DIDN'T INFORM HER OF WHAT SHE'D SAID UNDER HYPNOSIS.
BUT THIS ONE LITTLE DETAIL WAS A VERY TELLING PIECE OF INFORMATION.
IT TOLD ON YOU.

I SUPPLIED MISS LOCHER WITH A PROGRAM FOR SERENITY THAT INCLUDED VALIUM AND COMPANIONSHIP. (THE LATTER OF WHICH I ALSO RECOMMEND FOR US, DOLLING.)
I STILL WASN'T SURE IF SHE WAS A WILLING OR UNWILLING AGENT OF YOURS.
ISN'T IT POSSIBLE, SWEET LOVE, THAT HER INCREDIBLE DREAM WAS INDUCED BY ONE OF YOUR FAMED POST-HYPNOTIC SUGGESTIONS?
OR EVEN BY SO-CALLED "DREAM TELEPATHY" -- IN WHICH YOU HAVE NO SMALL INTEREST?
I REALIZE THAT PSYCHOLOGY HAS CHARTED SOME AWFULLY WEIRD AREAS IN ITS MAPS OF THE MIND. BUT YOU'VE GONE SO FAR INTO THE ULTRA-MENTAL HINTERLANDS OF METAPHYSICS THAT I FEAR YOU WILL NOT RETURN.
AT LEAST, NOT WITH YOUR REPUTATION INTACT.
WHAT **WERE** YOU DOING THE NIGHT MISS LOCHER UNDERWENT HER DREAM ORDEAL?
YOU WEREN'T WITH ME.
I KNOW THAT.

THE FOLLOWING WEEK, MISS LOCHER DID NOT APPEAR FOR HER APPOINTMENT.

WHEN I CALLED HER, THE PERSON WHO ANSWERED TOLD ME I HAD A WRONG NUMBER.

YOU WILL HAVE TO FORGIVE ME, MY LOVELY, IF BY THIS TIME I BEGAN TO FEEL LIKE THE VICTIM OF A HOAX. **YOUR** HOAX, TO BE EXACT.

I DECIDED TO CALL ON MISS LOCHER AT THE ADDRESS ON HER NEW PATIENT FORM.

THAT ADDRESS WAS IN A SHOPPING DISTRICT, PART OF A FASHIONABLE SUBURB ON THE OTHER SIDE OF TOWN.

BY THE TIME I ARRIVED, A STORM WAS IMMINENT AND THE AIR WAS APPROPRIATELY GALVANIZED WITH A PRE-DELUGE FEELING OF SUSPENSE.

OF COURSE, I NEED NOT DESCRIBE THE ATMOSPHERE OF A PLACE YOU'VE VISITED MANY TIMES, DEAR LOVE. BUT I WANTED TO SHOW HOW SENSITIVE I WAS TO THE MOOD, AND HOW RIPE I'D BECOME FOR THE STAGED ANTICS TO FOLLOW.

VERY GOOD, DOCTOR!

WHAT I DID NOT EXPECT WERE THE SHEER **LENGTHS** TO WHICH YOU WOULD GO. BUT ANYWAY, I SAW WHAT YOU WANTED ME TO SEE...

...OR WHAT I **THOUGHT** YOU WANTED ME TO SEE...

AS I SCANNED THE MANNIKIN'S FROZEN FACE, I NOTICED -- AS YOU CAN PROBABLY GUESS -- A CERTAIN MOISTNESS IN ITS FIXED GAZE...

PERHAPS I WAS SUBLIMINALLY LOOKING FOR A RESEMBLANCE TO MISS LOCHER.

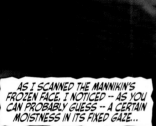

A SUDDEN SHOWER SENT ME RUNNING BACK TO MY CAR.

WHILE SITTING THERE -- WIPING MY RAIN-SPOTTED GLASSES --

-- I THOUGHT I SAW SOMETHING MOVE IN THE REAR-VIEW MIRROR.

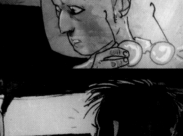

OF COURSE, THERE WAS NOTHING IN THE BACK SEAT.

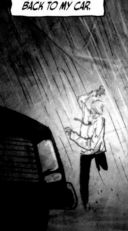

BUT THE POINT IS: YOU SUCCEEDED, MY LOVE, IN GETTING ME TO EXPERIENCE A MOMENT OF SELF-TERROR. AND HAVING CONFESSED THAT MUCH, I CAN NOW GET TO THE REAL FOCUS OF MY APPEAL TO YOU.

FOR THIS HAS FAR LESS TO DO WITH A. LOCHER, DEAREST, THAN IT DOES WITH US.

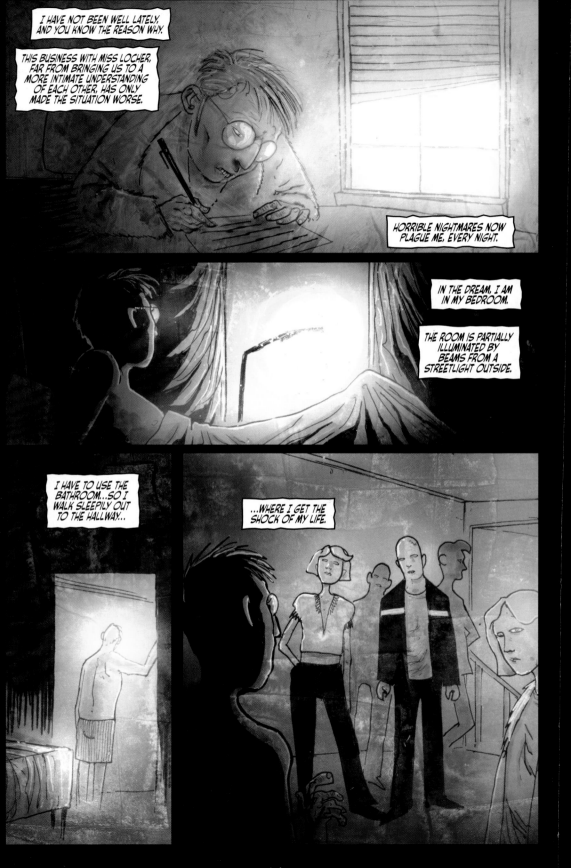

I HAVE NOT BEEN WELL LATELY, AND YOU KNOW THE REASON WHY.

THIS BUSINESS WITH MISS LOCHER, FAR FROM BRINGING US TO A MORE INTIMATE UNDERSTANDING OF EACH OTHER, HAS ONLY MADE THE SITUATION WORSE.

HORRIBLE NIGHTMARES NOW PLAGUE ME, EVERY NIGHT.

IN THE DREAM, I AM IN MY BEDROOM.

THE ROOM IS PARTIALLY ILLUMINATED BY BEAMS FROM A STREETLIGHT OUTSIDE.

I HAVE TO USE THE BATHROOM...SO I WALK SLEEPILY OUT TO THE HALLWAY...

...WHERE I GET THE SHOCK OF MY LIFE.

PEOPLE DRESSED AS DOLLS. OR DOLLS MADE UP TO LOOK LIKE PEOPLE.
PARALYZED WITH TERROR, I RETURN THEIR FIXED GAZE... WONDERING IF MY EYES ARE SHINING LIKE THEIRS.
THEN ONE OF THE DOLL-PEOPLE TURNS ITS HEAD HALTINGLY UPON A STIFF LITTLE NECK...
BECOME AS WE ARE, SWEETIE...
...DIE INTO US.
AFTER I AWAKE, SCREAMING, MY HEART POUNDS LIKE A MAD PRISONER INSIDE ME AND DOESN'T LET UP UNTIL MORNING.
YOU CAN HELP ME, SWEETHEART.
I KNOW YOU DIDN'T INTEND THIS, BUT THAT ELABORATE JOKE YOU PERPETRATED WITH THE HELP OF MISS LOCHER HAS REALLY GOTTEN TO ME.
PLEASE, RELEASE ME FROM YOUR SPELL... AND LET'S BEGIN A **NORMAL** ROMANCE.

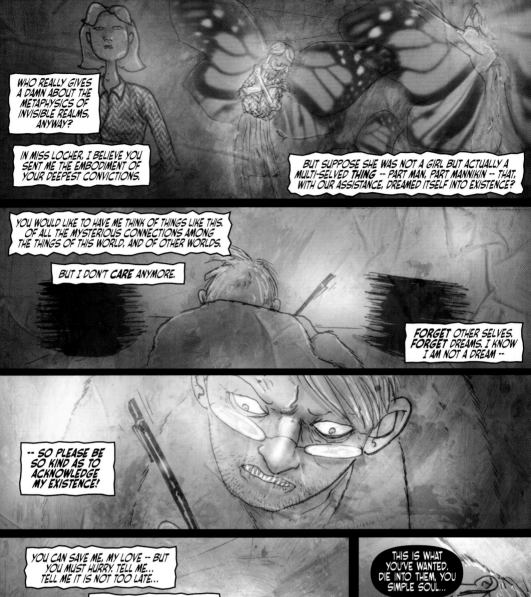

WHO REALLY GIVES A DAMN ABOUT THE METAPHYSICS OF INVISIBLE REALMS, ANYWAY?

IN MISS LOCHER, I BELIEVE YOU SENT ME THE EMBODIMENT OF YOUR DEEPEST CONVICTIONS.

BUT SUPPOSE SHE WAS NOT A GIRL BUT ACTUALLY A MULTI-SELVED *THING* -- PART MAN, PART MANNIKIN -- THAT, WITH OUR ASSISTANCE, DREAMED ITSELF INTO EXISTENCE?

YOU WOULD LIKE TO HAVE ME THINK OF THINGS LIKE THIS. OF ALL THE MYSTERIOUS CONNECTIONS AMONG THE THINGS OF THIS WORLD, AND OF OTHER WORLDS.

BUT I DON'T *CARE* ANYMORE.

FORGET OTHER SELVES. FORGET DREAMS. I KNOW I AM NOT A DREAM --

-- SO PLEASE BE SO KIND AS TO ACKNOWLEDGE MY EXISTENCE!

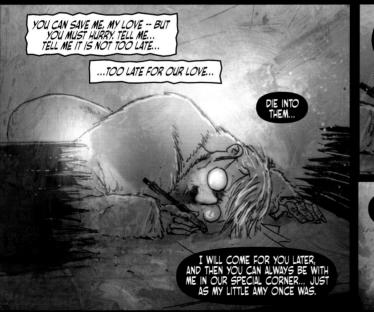

YOU CAN SAVE ME, MY LOVE -- BUT YOU MUST HURRY. TELL ME... TELL ME IT IS NOT TOO LATE...

...TOO LATE FOR OUR LOVE...

DIE INTO THEM...

I WILL COME FOR YOU LATER, AND THEN YOU CAN ALWAYS BE WITH ME IN OUR SPECIAL CORNER... JUST AS MY LITTLE AMY ONCE WAS.

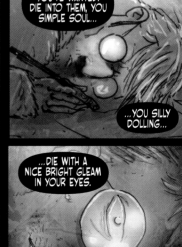

THIS IS WHAT YOU'VE WANTED. DIE INTO THEM, YOU SIMPLE SOUL...

...YOU SILLY DOLLING...

...DIE WITH A NICE BRIGHT GLEAM IN YOUR EYES.

THE END

48

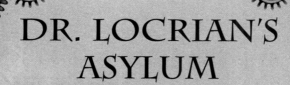

DR. LOCRIAN'S ASYLUM

There is a longtime connection between madness and supernatural horror. A fractured mind is often the way in to a world not suspected by those of an innocent normality. Reciprocally, the supernatural may invade our world through a doorway provided by a mangled brain. A fine recent example of this two-way street has been shown to us in the film *Session 9*, wherein a crew of men cleaning up an abandoned mental institution find themselves crossing the line where reason and reality are both out of balance. In this instance, none of the men make it back to business as usual. An earlier example of the special relationship between the insane and the supernatural is featured in Bram Stoker's *Dracula*. How natural it seems that an inmate of Dr. Seward's asylum named Renfield should be in league with the bloodsucker that has come to visit the coastal town of Whitby, England.

While belief in the supernatural is only superstition, the *sense* of the supernatural cannot be denied. And that sense is often among the symptoms of the psychically perturbed. It is the sense of what *should not be* at its most potent, the sense of the impossible that most of us experience in our dreams and the madman knows while he is awake. Not that the rest of us are immune from being overtaken by otherworldly fears, for we also have brains. And where there is a brain, there is a ready, and sometimes willing, victim of imaginings beyond the edge of everyday existence. We even inflict these ventures of a superstitious delirium on ourselves, certifying the abnormality of human consciousness every time we subject our rational sensibilities to unsound fictions. After all, what could be more deranged than to pay for the privilege of committing our imaginations to places where the dead return from their graves in the form of ghosts, vampires, zombies, and what have you; where demons can move into bodies and change them in awful ways; where things we never imagined can drop out of the darkness like so many spiders from their webs; where what seemed so right can become so terribly wrong in a mere moment; and where anything, including the world itself, may be wearing a mask behind which it hides its true horror.

The supernatural may be considered as the metaphysical counterpart of insanity and, as such, is the hallmark of the uncanny nightmare of a conscious mind marooned for a brief while in this haunted house of a universe and being driven mad by the ghastliness of it all. This viewpoint is sourced in a dementia symptomatic of our life as transients in a world that is natural for all else that lives, yet, by our lights, when they are not flickering or gone out, is anything but. The most phenomenal of creaturely traits, the sense of the supernatural, the impression of a fatal estrangement from the visible, is dependent on our minds, which immerse the sane and the straight-jacketed alike in a cosmic comedy without laughter. It is in our heads that ground is always being broken for the building of *Dr. Locrian's Asylum*.

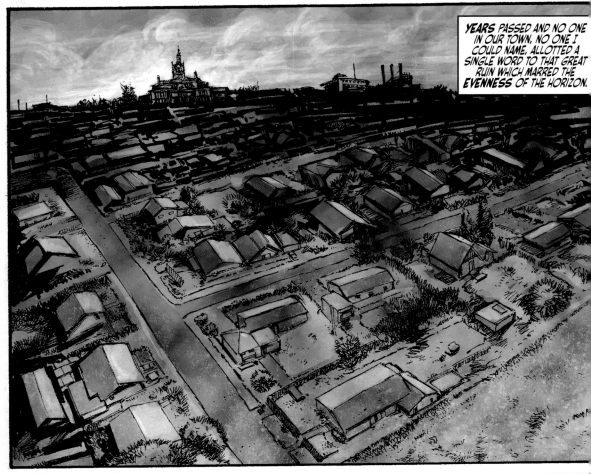

YEARS PASSED AND NO ONE IN OUR TOWN, NO ONE I COULD NAME, ALLOTTED A SINGLE WORD TO THAT GREAT RUIN WHICH MARRED THE *EVENNESS* OF THE HORIZON.

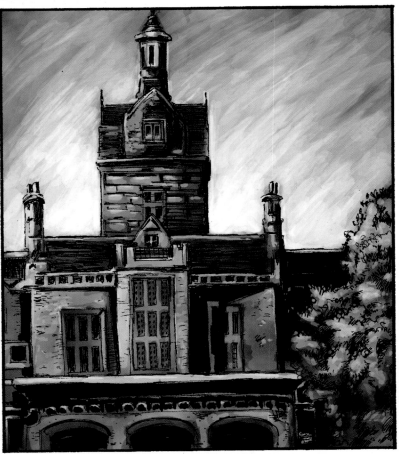

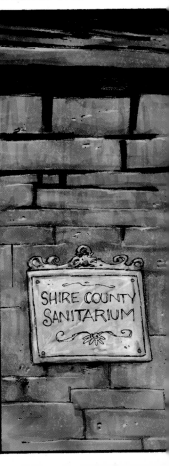

SHIRE COUNTY SANITARIUM

PLEASE... D-DON'T...
I WON'T TELL A SOUL...
IT'LL BE OUR SECRET..
...OUR SECRET...IT'LL BE SAFE...
...WITH ME...

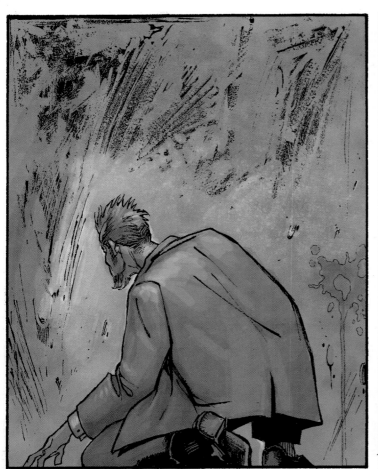

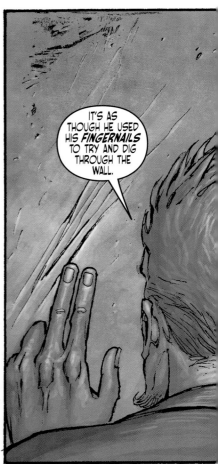

IT'S AS THOUGH HE USED HIS *FINGERNAILS* TO TRY AND DIG THROUGH THE WALL.

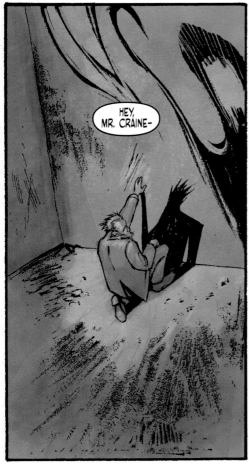

HEY, MR. CRAINE—

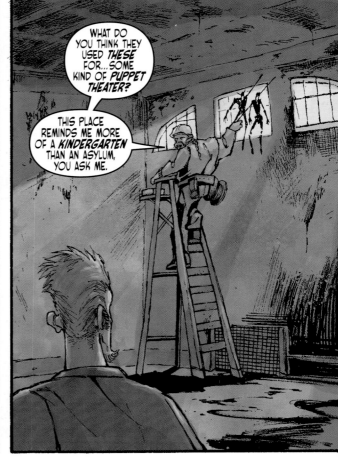

WHAT DO YOU THINK THEY USED *THESE* FOR...SOME KIND OF *PUPPET THEATER?*

THIS PLACE REMINDS ME MORE OF A *KINDERGARTEN* THAN AN ASYLUM, YOU ASK ME.

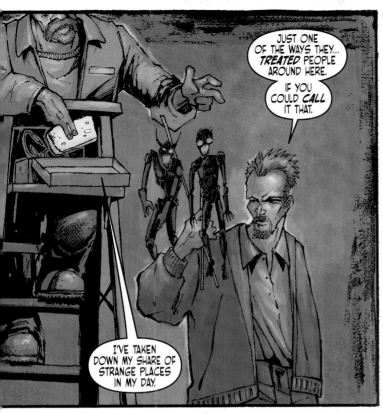

JUST ONE OF THE WAYS THEY... *TREATED* PEOPLE AROUND HERE.

IF YOU COULD *CALL* IT THAT.

I'VE TAKEN DOWN MY SHARE OF STRANGE PLACES IN MY DAY.

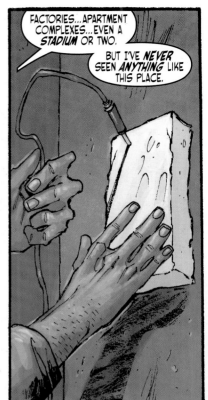

FACTORIES... APARTMENT COMPLEXES... EVEN A *STADIUM* OR TWO.

BUT I'VE *NEVER* SEEN *ANYTHING* LIKE THIS PLACE.

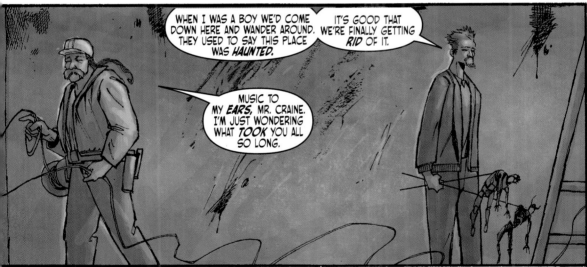

WHEN I WAS A BOY WE'D COME DOWN HERE AND WANDER AROUND. THEY USED TO SAY THIS PLACE WAS *HAUNTED*.

IT'S GOOD THAT WE'RE FINALLY GETTING *RID* OF IT.

MUSIC TO MY *EARS*, MR. CRAINE. I'M JUST WONDERING WHAT *TOOK* YOU ALL SO LONG.

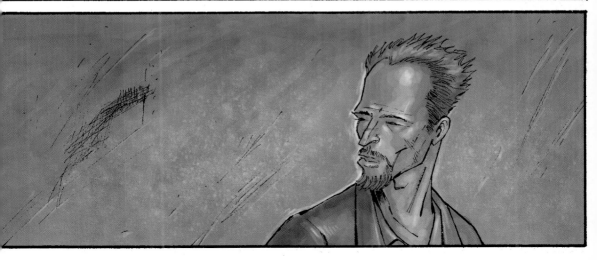

PERHAPS SOMEONE *HAD* PROPOSED TEARING *DOWN* THE OLD ASYLUM EARLIER AND RAZING ITS ADJACENT *BURIAL GROUND,* WHERE NO INMATE HAD BEEN INTERRED FOR A GENERATION OR MORE.

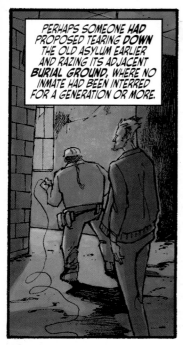

BUT THOUGH WE WERE ALL *HAUNTED* BY THE *SAME REVENANT,* THE RESOLUTION HAD ALWAYS APPEARED POORLY *FORMED.*

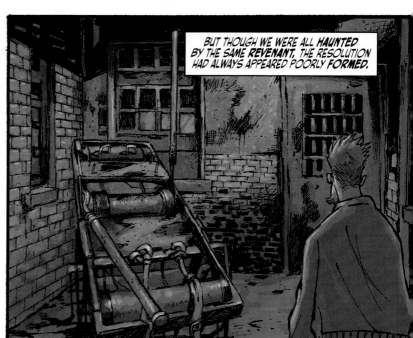

UM... MR. CRAINE?

HM?

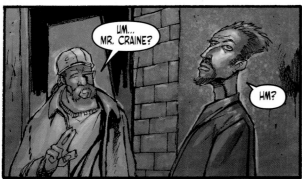

YOU MIGHT WANT TO WEAR THIS.

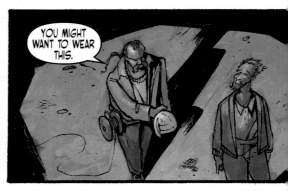

THEN HOW CAN I EXPLAIN THE *SUDDEN* TURN OF EVENTS, THAT OVERNIGHT *CONVERSION* WHICH SET OUR STEPS TOWARD THAT HULKING AND DECAYED *EDIFICE—*

—TRAMPLING ITS *GRAVEYARD* ALONG THE WAY?

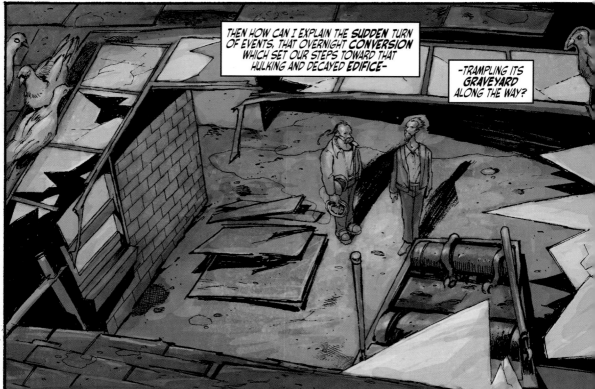

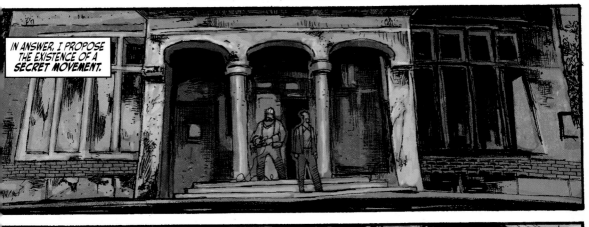

IN ANSWER, I PROPOSE THE EXISTENCE OF A *SECRET MOVEMENT.*

ONE CONDUCTED IN THE *SOULS* OF THE TOWN'S CITIZENS.

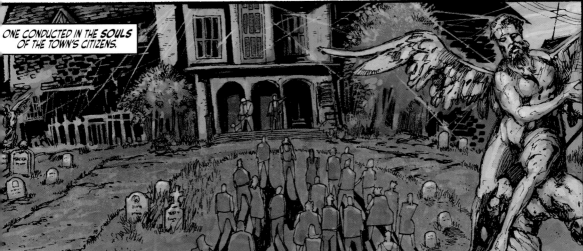

AND IN THEIR *DREAMS.*

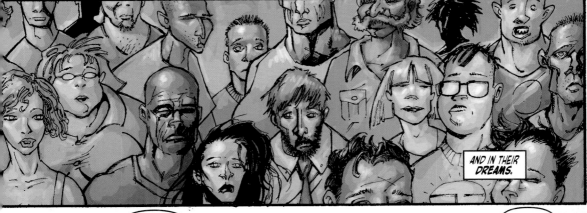

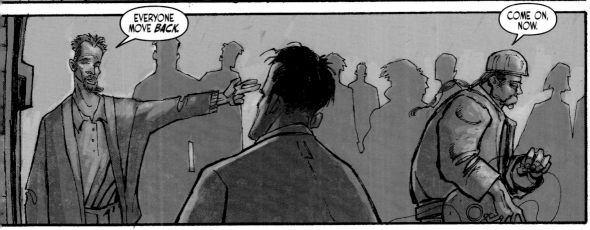

EVERYONE MOVE *BACK.*

COME ON, NOW.

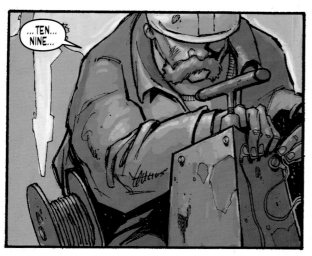

...TEN... NINE...

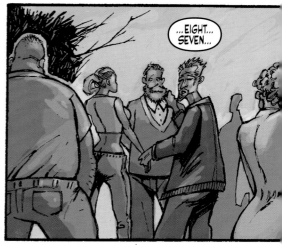

...EIGHT... SEVEN...

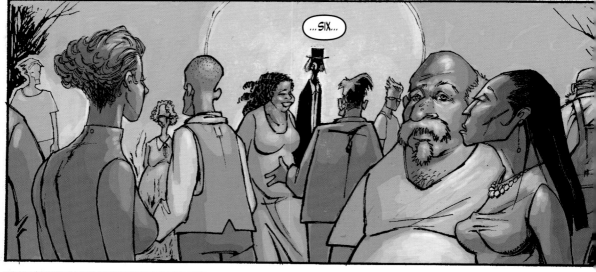

...SIX...

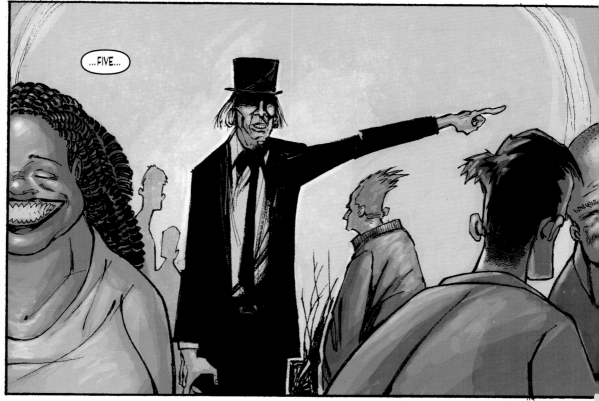

...FIVE...

WHAT-?
.FOUR...
WAIT...
...THREE...
...TWO...
DON'T--!
...ONE

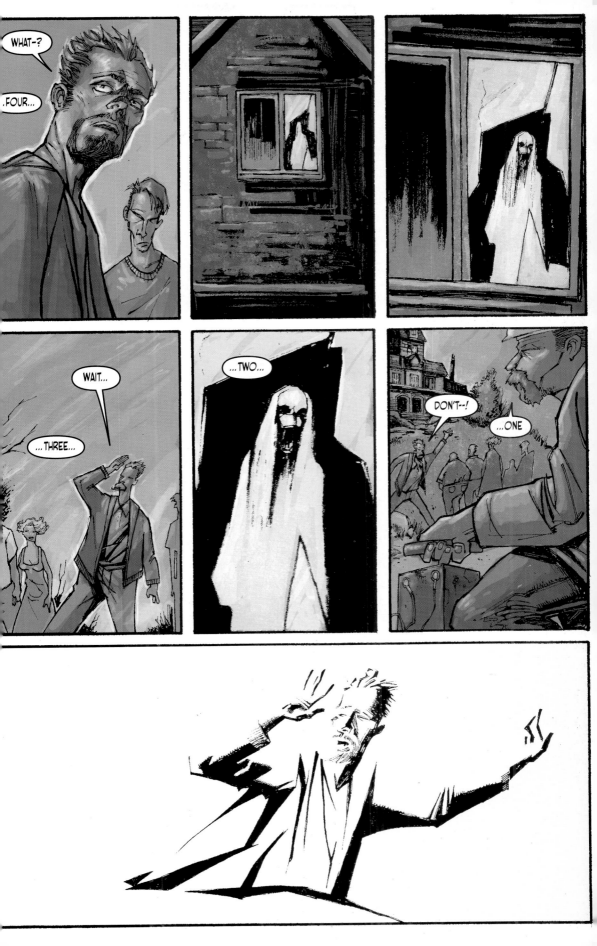

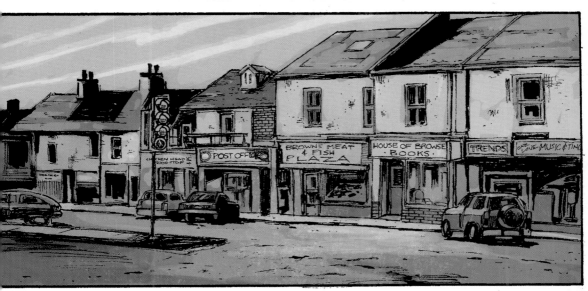

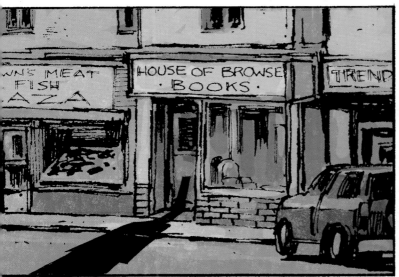

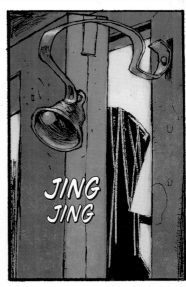

JING
JING

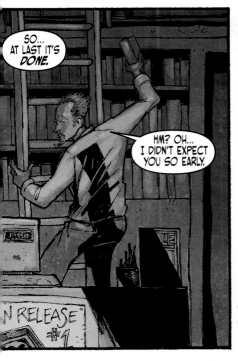

SO...
AT LAST IT'S
DONE.

HM? OH...
I DIDN'T EXPECT
YOU SO EARLY.

N RELEASE
#1

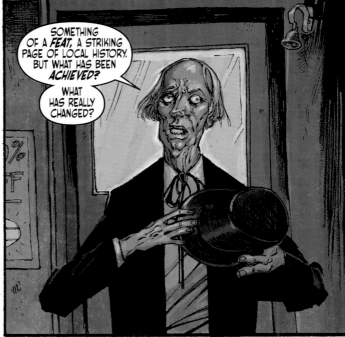

SOMETHING
OF A *FEAT*, A STRIKING
PAGE OF LOCAL HISTORY.
BUT WHAT HAS BEEN
ACHIEVED?

WHAT
HAS REALLY
CHANGED?

IF YOU MEAN THAT THERE'S VERY LITTLE DIFFERENCE NOW, I WOULD HAVE TO AGREE.
WE ONLY INTENDED TO REMOVE AN EYESORE.
WE MUST BE WALKING DIFFERENT STREETS, MR. CRAINE...
...AND SEEING QUITE DIFFERENT FACES...HEARING DIFFERENT VOICES IN THIS TOWN.
ON MY WAY OVER, I HEARD SOME PEOPLE SAYING THINGS THEY DID NOT THINK I COULD HEAR.
SOMEHOW EVERYONE SEEMS TO KNOW ABOUT THESE BOOKS OF MINE, MR. CRAINE.
I - I'M SORRY. I DIDN'T INTEND TO VIOLATE ANY CONFIDENCE.
NEW RELEASE #1
SKULL
NOW ON SALE
TELL ME, DID YOU EVER HEAR THOSE STORIES ABOUT THE SANITARIUM?
WHAT SOME PEOPLE SAW IN ITS WINDOWS?

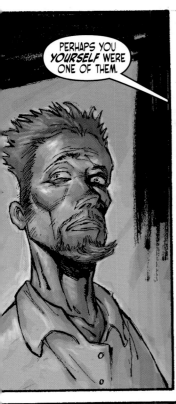

PERHAPS YOU *YOURSELF* WERE ONE OF THEM.

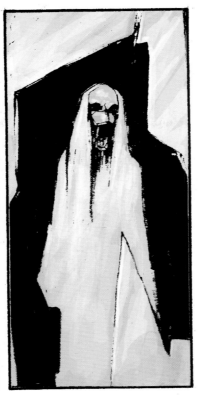

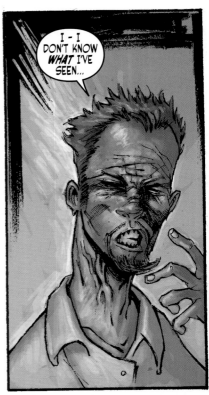

I - I DON'T KNOW *WHAT* I'VE SEEN...

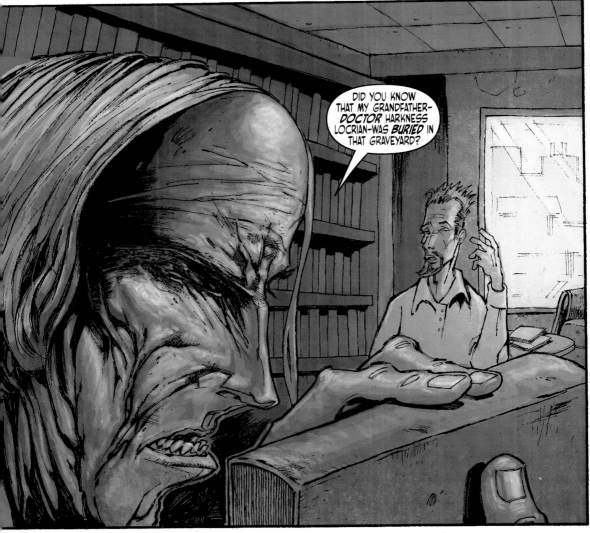

DID YOU KNOW THAT MY GRANDFATHER— *DOCTOR* HARKNESS LOCRIAN—WAS *BURIED* IN THAT GRAVEYARD?

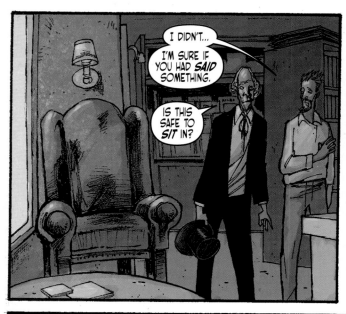

I DIDN'T... I'M SURE IF YOU HAD *SAID* SOMETHING.

IS THIS SAFE TO *SIT* IN?

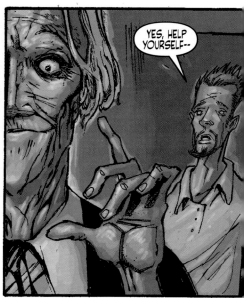

YES, HELP YOURSELF--

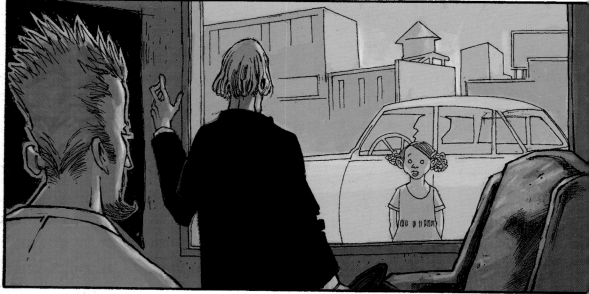

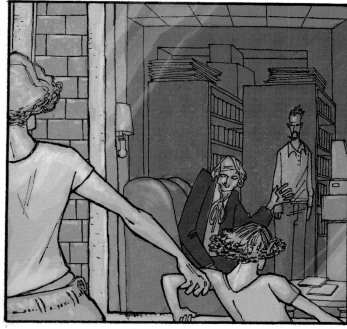

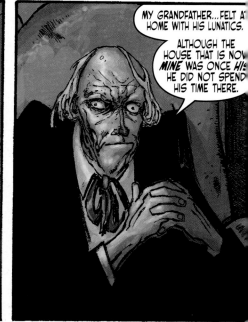

MY GRANDFATHER...FELT AT HOME WITH HIS LUNATICS.

ALTHOUGH THE HOUSE THAT IS NOW *MINE* WAS ONCE *HIS,* HE DID NOT SPEND HIS TIME THERE.

IT WAS ONLY AFTER THEY *CLOSED DOWN* THE SANITARIUM THAT HE ACTUALLY BECAME A *RESIDENT* OF HIS OWN HOME.

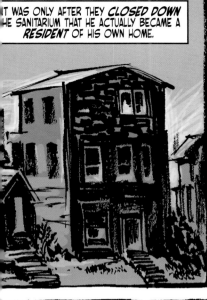

"MY GRANDFATHER PASSED HIS FINAL YEARS IN THE SMALL UPSTAIRS ROOM OVERLOOKING THE OUTSKIRTS OF TOWN.

"I RECALL SEEING HIM, DAY AFTER DAY, GAZING THROUGH HIS WINDOW AT THE *SANITARIUM.*

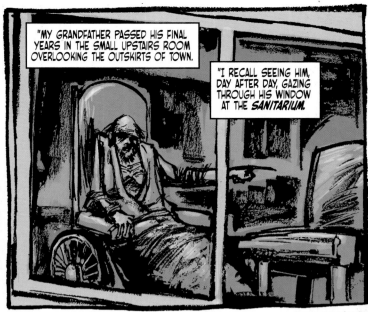

"HIS FEELINGS WITH RESPECT TO THE SANITARIUM WERE QUITE INCREDIBLE, OWING TO THE MANNER IN WHICH HE HAD USED HIS *AUTHORITY* IN THAT PLACE.

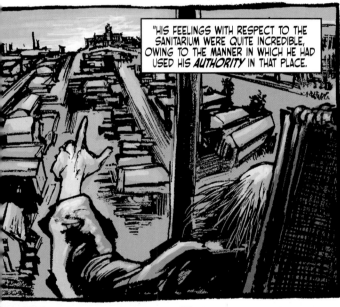

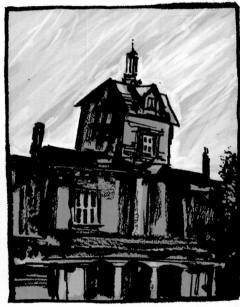

I DISREGARDED MY PARENTS' *ADMONITIONS* THAT I NOT SPEND TOO MUCH TIME WITH THE OLD MAN, SUCCUMBING TO THE *MYSTERY* OF HIS PRESENCE.

"AND ONE AFTERNOON HE REVEALED HIMSELF..."

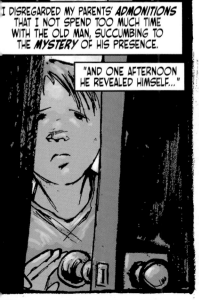

THEY QUESTIONED...

THEY ACCUSED...

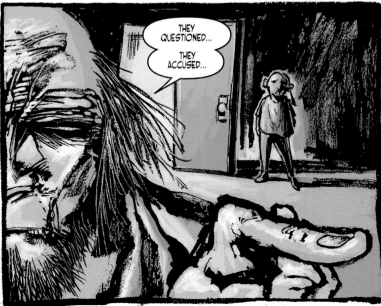

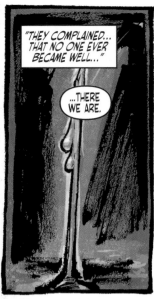

"THEY COMPLAINED... THAT NO ONE EVER BECAME WELL..."

...THERE WE ARE.

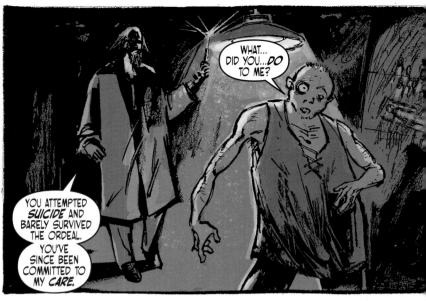

WHAT... DID YOU...*DO* TO ME?

YOU ATTEMPTED *SUICIDE* AND BARELY SURVIVED THE ORDEAL.

YOU'VE SINCE BEEN COMMITTED TO MY *CARE.*

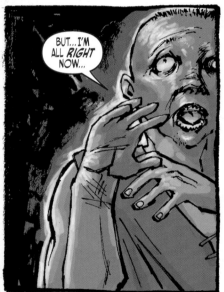

BUT...I'M ALL *RIGHT* NOW...

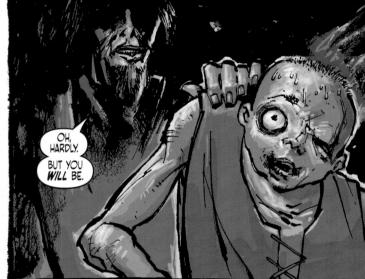

OH, HARDLY.

BUT YOU *WILL* BE.

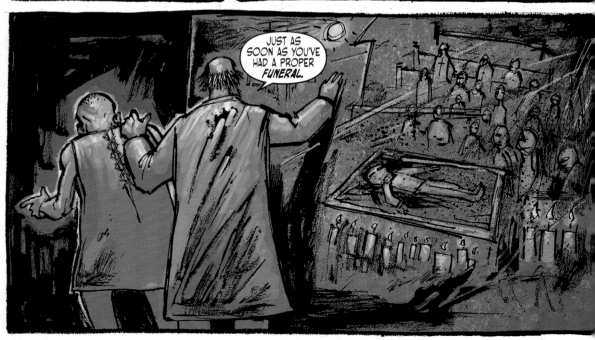

JUST AS SOON AS YOU'VE HAD A PROPER *FUNERAL.*

WHERE DID...
BUT...
YOU HAVE TO LISTEN TO ME. CHRIST...
I'VE CHANGED MY MIND...I WANT TO LIVE...
OH GOD...OH MY GOD, HELP ME...
PLEASE...
I'M NOT... DEAD...

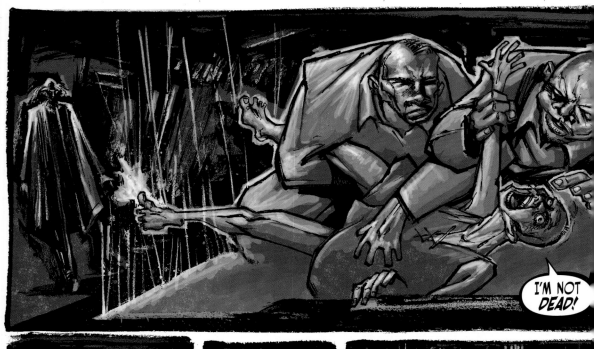

I'M NOT *DEAD!*

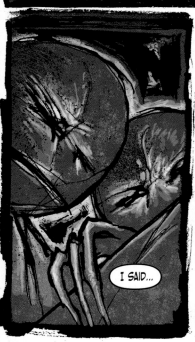

I SAID...

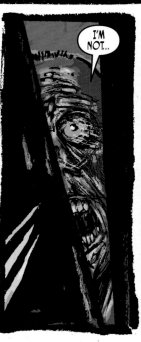

I'M NOT...

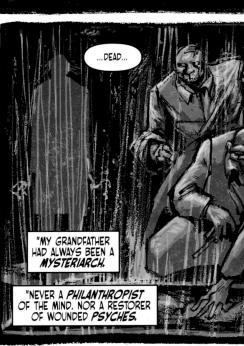

...DEAD...

"MY GRANDFATHER HAD ALWAYS BEEN A *MYSTERIARCH.*

"NEVER A *PHILANTHROPIST* OF THE MIND. NOR A RESTORER OF WOUNDED *PSYCHES.*

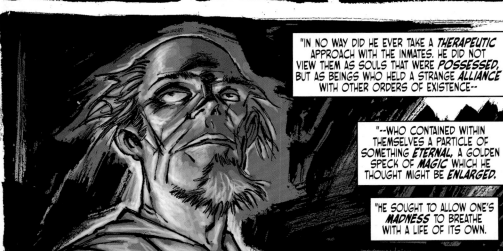

"IN NO WAY DID HE EVER TAKE A *THERAPEUTIC* APPROACH WITH THE INMATES. HE DID NOT VIEW THEM AS SOULS THAT WERE *POSSESSED,* BUT AS BEINGS WHO HELD A STRANGE *ALLIANCE* WITH OTHER ORDERS OF EXISTENCE--

"--WHO CONTAINED WITHIN THEMSELVES A PARTICLE OF SOMETHING *ETERNAL,* A GOLDEN SPECK OF *MAGIC* WHICH HE THOUGHT MIGHT BE *ENLARGED.*

"HE SOUGHT TO ALLOW ONE'S *MADNESS* TO BREATHE WITH A LIFE OF ITS OWN.

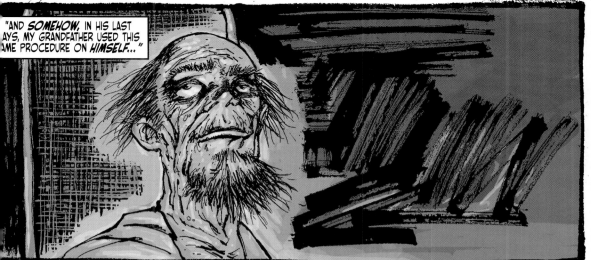

"AND *SOMEHOW,* IN HIS LAST DAYS, MY GRANDFATHER USED THIS SAME PROCEDURE ON *HIMSELF...*"

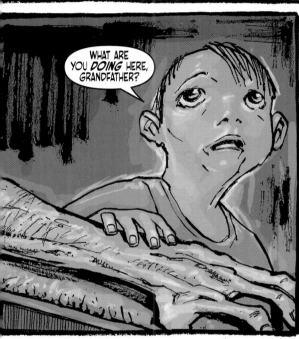

WHAT ARE YOU *DOING* HERE, GRANDFATHER?

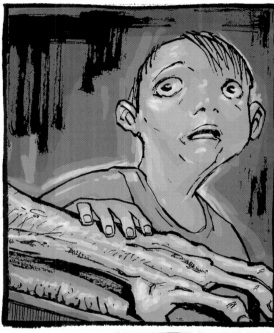

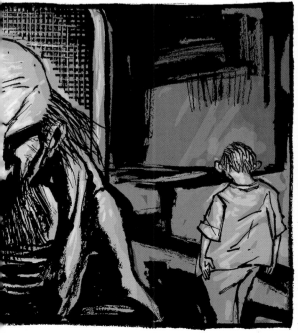

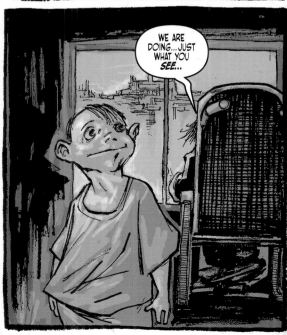

WE ARE DOING... JUST WHAT YOU *SEE...*

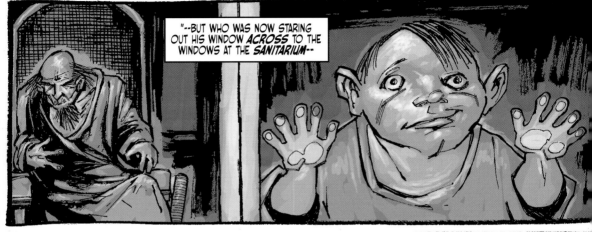

"WHAT I SAW WAS AN OLD MAN WHO BELONGED IN THE *GRAVE*--

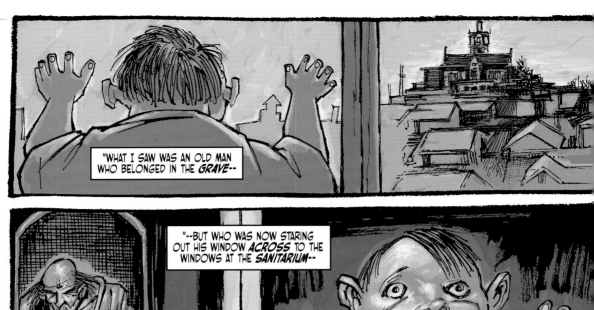

"--BUT WHO WAS NOW STARING OUT HIS WINDOW *ACROSS* TO THE WINDOWS AT THE *SANITARIUM*--

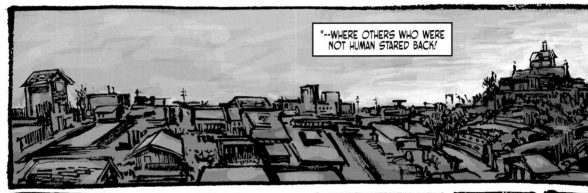

"--WHERE OTHERS WHO WERE NOT HUMAN STARED BACK!

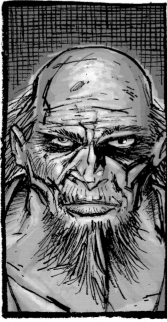
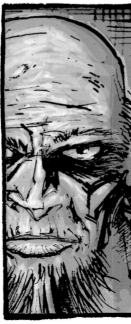
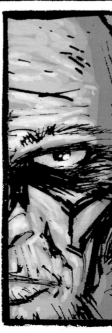
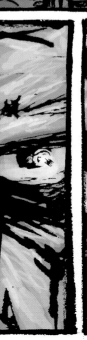

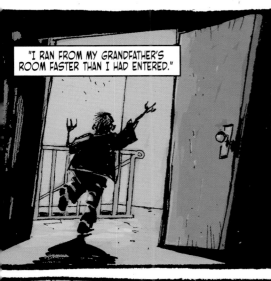

"I RAN FROM MY GRANDFATHER'S ROOM FASTER THAN I HAD ENTERED."

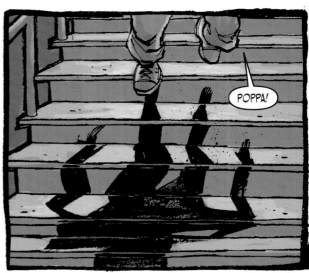

POPPA!

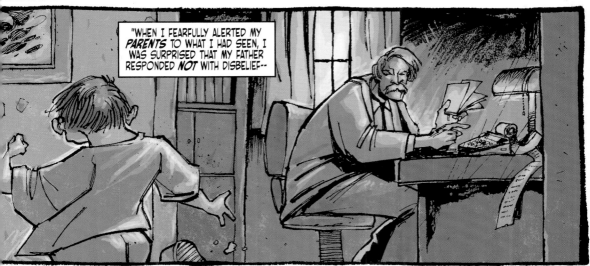

"WHEN I FEARFULLY ALERTED MY PARENTS TO WHAT I HAD SEEN, I WAS SURPRISED THAT MY FATHER RESPONDED NOT WITH DISBELIEF--

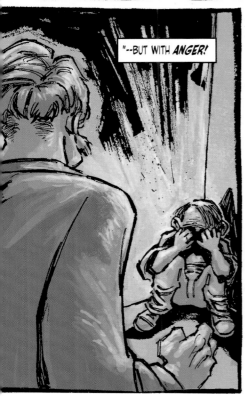

"--BUT WITH ANGER!"

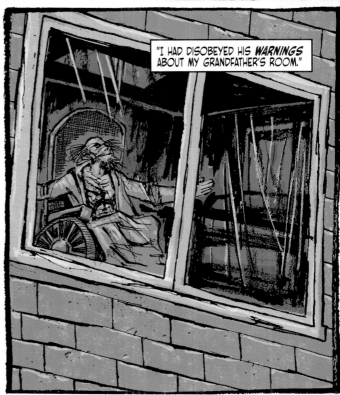

"I HAD DISOBEYED HIS WARNINGS ABOUT MY GRANDFATHER'S ROOM."

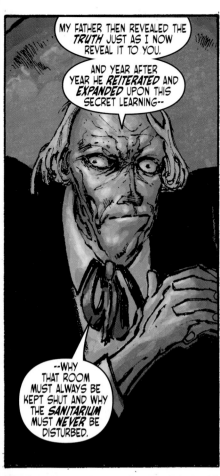

MY FATHER THEN REVEALED THE *TRUTH* JUST AS I NOW REVEAL IT TO YOU.

AND YEAR AFTER YEAR HE *REITERATED* AND *EXPANDED* UPON THIS SECRET LEARNING--

--WHY THAT ROOM MUST ALWAYS BE KEPT SHUT AND WHY THE *SANITARIUM* MUST *NEVER* BE DISTURBED.

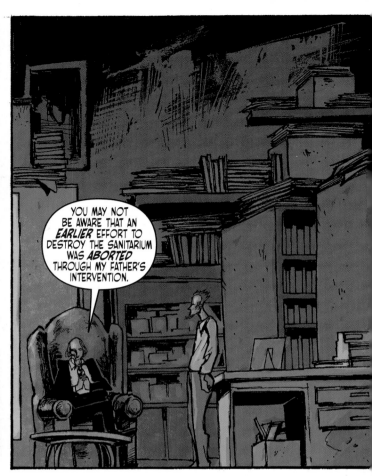

YOU MAY NOT BE AWARE THAT AN *EARLIER* EFFORT TO DESTROY THE SANITARIUM WAS *ABORTED* THROUGH MY FATHER'S INTERVENTION.

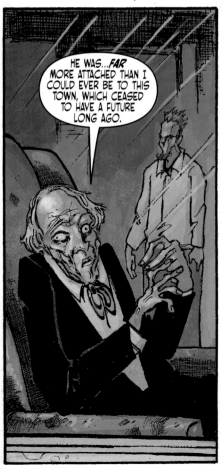

HE WAS...*FAR* MORE ATTACHED THAN I COULD EVER BE TO THIS TOWN, WHICH CEASED TO HAVE A FUTURE LONG AGO.

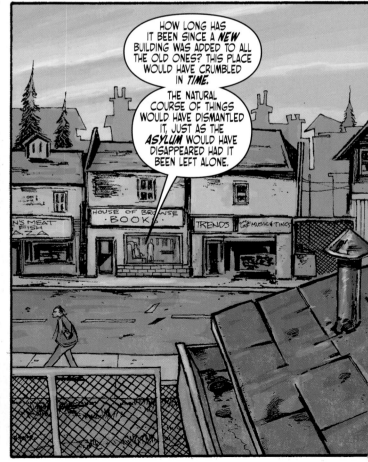

HOW LONG HAS IT BEEN SINCE A *NEW* BUILDING WAS ADDED TO ALL THE OLD ONES? THIS PLACE WOULD HAVE CRUMBLED IN *TIME*.

THE NATURAL COURSE OF THINGS WOULD HAVE DISMANTLED IT, JUST AS THE *ASYLUM* WOULD HAVE DISAPPEARED HAD IT BEEN LEFT ALONE.

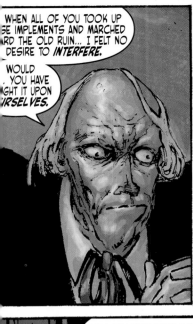

WHEN ALL OF YOU TOOK UP [THE]SE IMPLEMENTS AND MARCHED [TOWA]RD THE OLD RUIN... I FELT NO DESIRE TO *INTERFERE*.

[I] WOULD [THINK] YOU HAVE [BROU]GHT IT UPON [YOU]RSELVES.

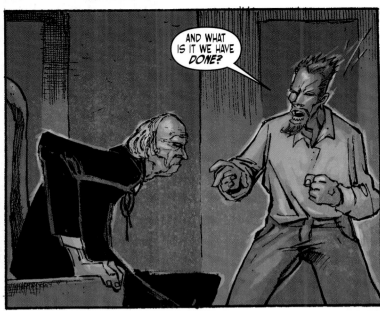

AND WHAT IS IT WE HAVE *DONE?*

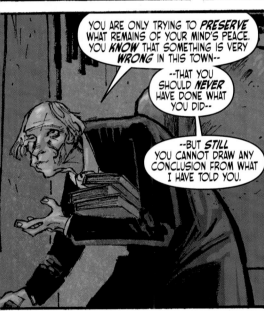

YOU ARE ONLY TRYING TO *PRESERVE* WHAT REMAINS OF YOUR MIND'S PEACE. YOU *KNOW* THAT SOMETHING IS VERY *WRONG* IN THIS TOWN--

--THAT YOU SHOULD *NEVER* HAVE DONE WHAT YOU DID--

--BUT *STILL* YOU CANNOT DRAW ANY CONCLUSION FROM WHAT I HAVE TOLD YOU.

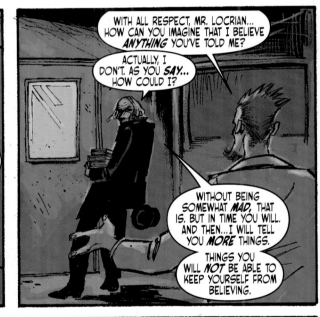

WITH ALL RESPECT, MR. LOCRIAN... HOW CAN YOU IMAGINE THAT I BELIEVE *ANYTHING* YOU'VE TOLD ME?

ACTUALLY, I DON'T, AS YOU *SAY...* HOW COULD I?

WITHOUT BEING SOMEWHAT *MAD*, THAT IS. BUT IN TIME YOU WILL. AND THEN...I WILL TELL YOU *MORE* THINGS.

THINGS YOU WILL *NOT* BE ABLE TO KEEP YOURSELF FROM BELIEVING.

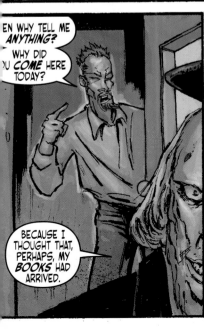

[TH]EN WHY TELL ME [ME] *ANYTHING?*

WHY DID [YO]U *COME* HERE TODAY?

BECAUSE I THOUGHT THAT, PERHAPS, MY *BOOKS* HAD ARRIVED.

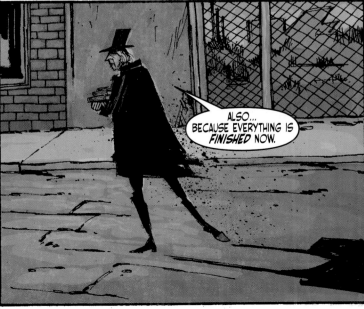

ALSO... BECAUSE EVERYTHING IS *FINISHED* NOW.

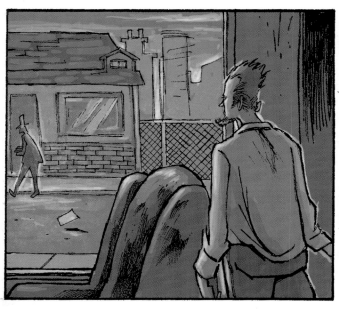
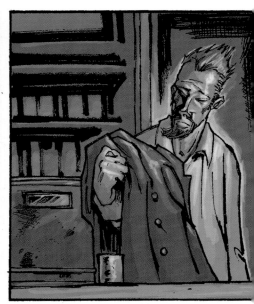
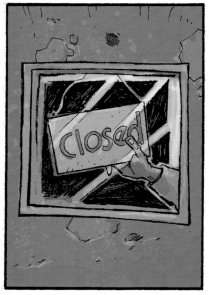
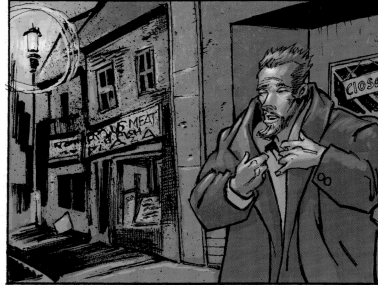
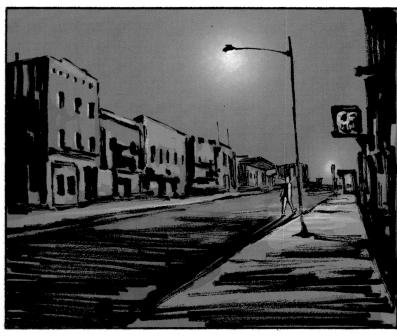
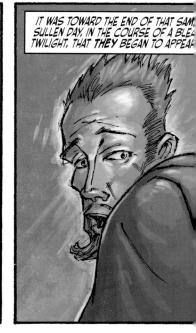

IT WAS TOWARD THE END OF THAT SAM, SULLEN DAY, IN THE COURSE OF A BLE. TWILIGHT, THAT **THEY** BEGAN TO APPEA.

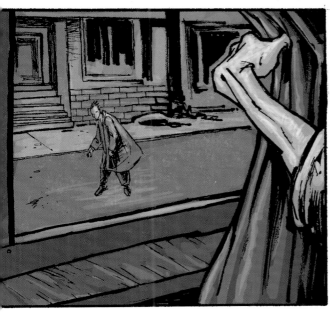

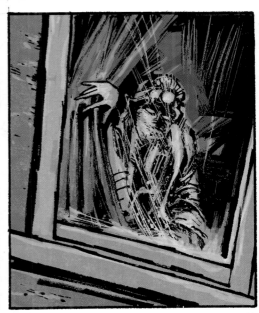

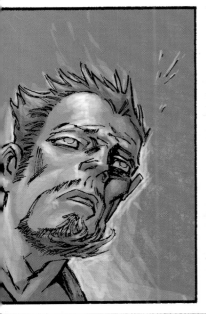

BY NIGHTFALL, THEY WERE DISTRACTINGLY **CONSPICUOUS** THROUGHOUT THE TOWN, ALWAYS FRAMED IN SOME **HIGH WINDOW** OF THE STRUCTURES THEY OCCUPIED--

THE ROOMS ABOVE THE SHOPS IN THE HEART OF TOWN.

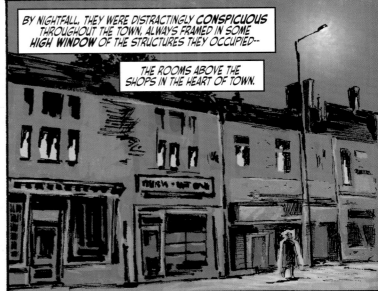

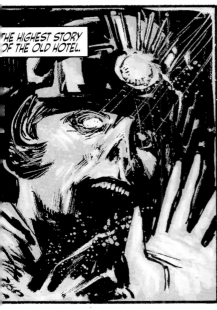

THE HIGHEST STORY OF THE OLD HOTEL.

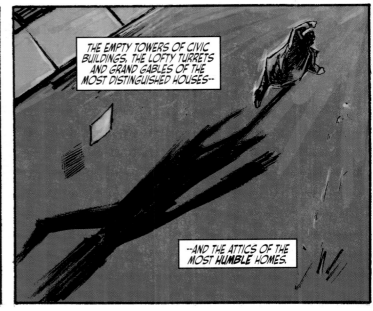

THE EMPTY TOWERS OF CIVIC BUILDINGS, THE LOFTY TURRETS AND GRAND GABLES OF THE MOST DISTINGUISHED HOUSES--

--AND THE ATTICS OF THE MOST **HUMBLE** HOMES.

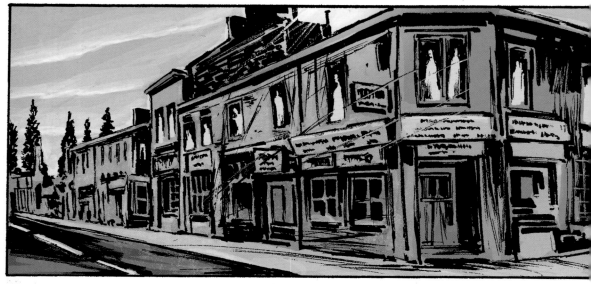

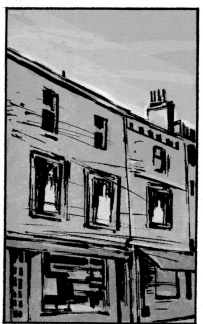

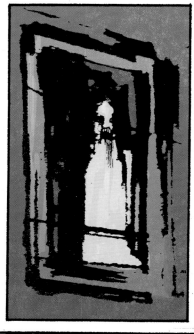

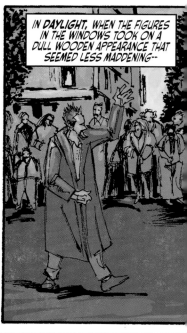

IN *DAYLIGHT,* WHEN THE FIGURES IN THE WINDOWS TOOK ON A DULL WOODEN APPEARANCE THAT SEEMED LESS MADDENING--

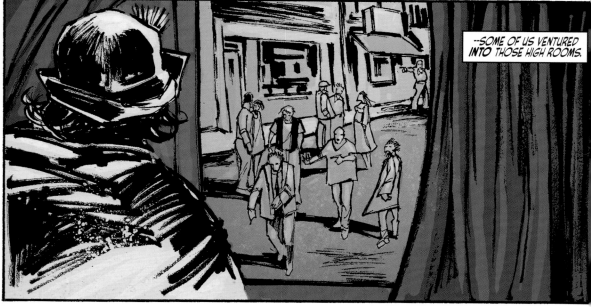

--SOME OF US VENTURED INTO THOSE HIGH ROOMS.

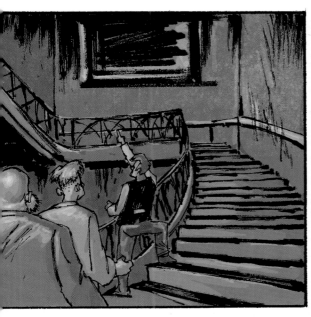
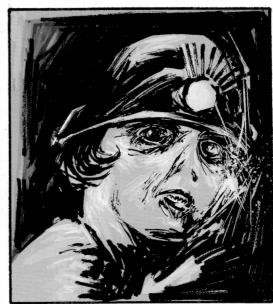
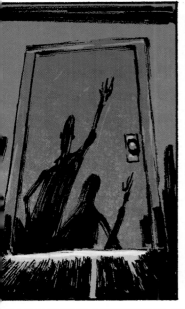
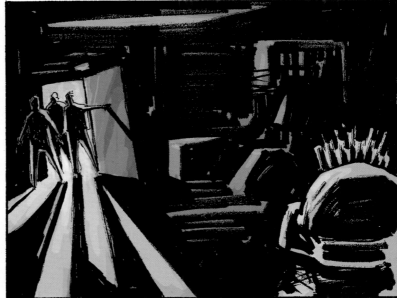
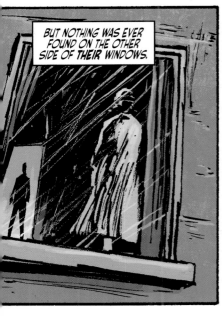

BUT NOTHING WAS EVER FOUND ON THE OTHER SIDE OF *THEIR* WINDOWS.

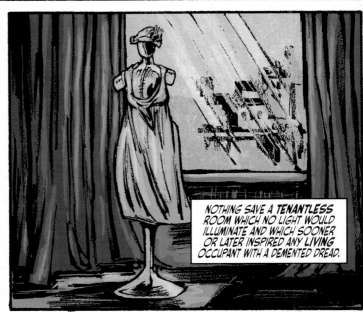

NOTHING SAVE A *TENANTLESS* ROOM WHICH NO LIGHT WOULD ILLUMINATE AND WHICH SOONER OR LATER INSPIRED ANY *LIVING* OCCUPANT WITH A DEMENTED DREAD.

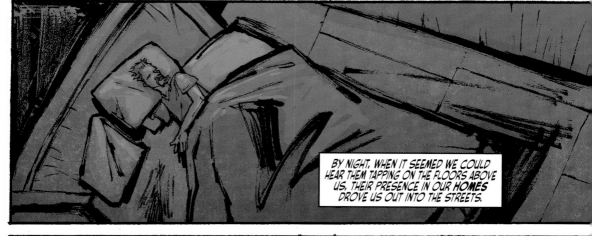

BY NIGHT, WHEN IT SEEMED WE COULD HEAR THEM TAPPING ON THE FLOORS ABOVE US, THEIR PRESENCE IN OUR **HOMES** DROVE US OUT INTO THE STREETS.

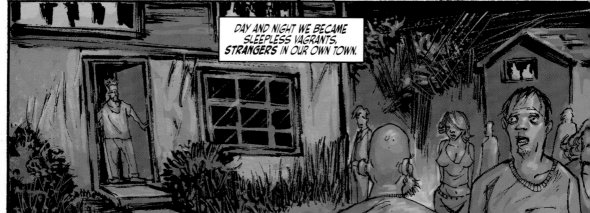

DAY AND NIGHT WE BECAME SLEEPLESS VAGRANTS, **STRANGERS** IN OUR OWN TOWN.

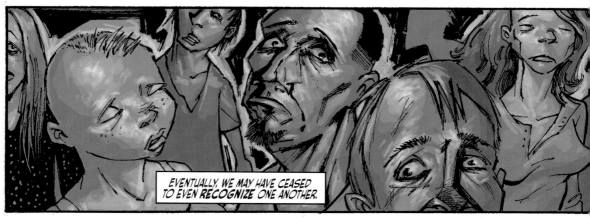

EVENTUALLY, WE MAY HAVE CEASED TO EVEN **RECOGNIZE** ONE ANOTHER.

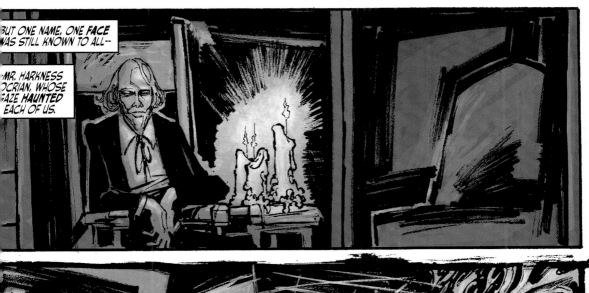

BUT ONE NAME, ONE *FACE* WAS STILL KNOWN TO ALL--

--MR. HARKNESS DORIAN, WHOSE GAZE *HAUNTED* EACH OF US.

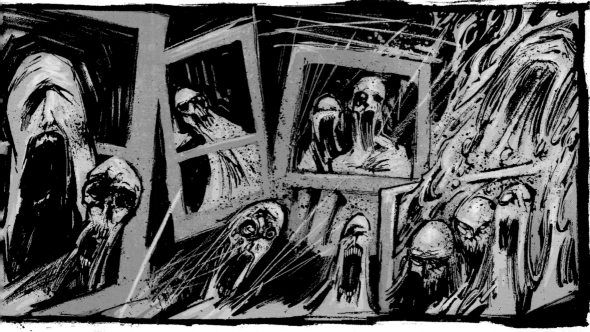

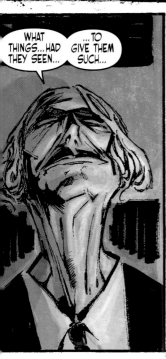

WHAT THINGS...HAD THEY SEEN...

....TO GIVE THEM SUCH...

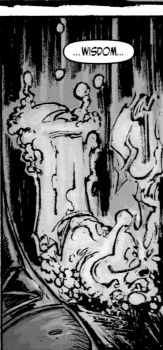

...WISDOM...

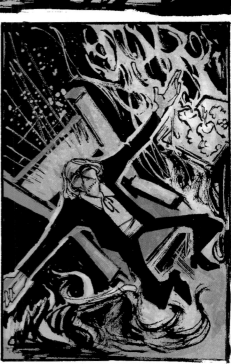

THE FIRE SPREAD,
MINDLESSLY CONSUMING
EVERY CORNER OF THE TOWN.

THERE WERE **ATTEMPTS** MADE TO
OPPOSE ITS PATH, BUT THEY WERE
HALF-HEARTED AND SOON ABANDONED.

FOR THE MOST PART, WE STOOD IN
SILENCE, VACANTLY STARING AS THE
FLAMES BURNED THEIR WAY UP TO THE
HIGH **WINDOWS** WHERE SPECTRAL FIGURES
POSED LIKE **PORTRAITS** IN THEIR FRAMES.

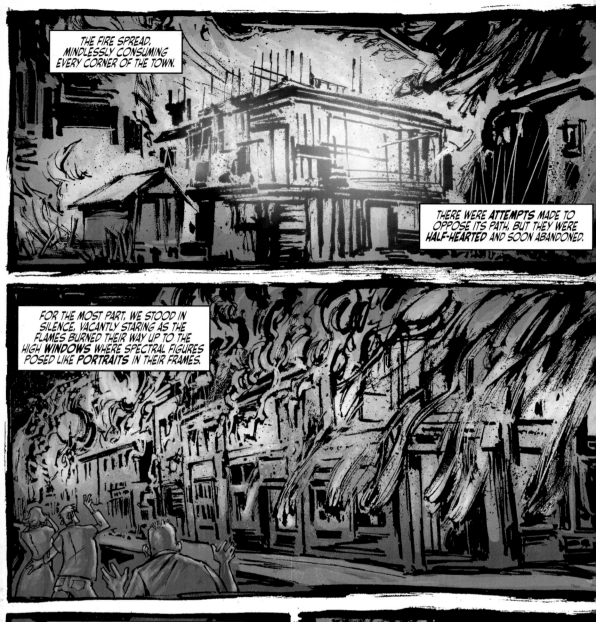

ULTIMATELY THESE DEMONS WERE
EXORCISED...BUT ONLY **AFTER** THE TOWN HAD
BEEN ANNULLED BY THE **HOLOCAUST.**

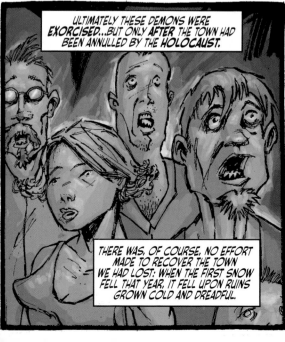

THERE WAS, OF COURSE, NO EFFORT
MADE TO RECOVER THE TOWN
WE HAD LOST: WHEN THE FIRST SNOW
FELL THAT YEAR, IT FELL UPON RUINS
GROWN COLD AND DREADFUL.

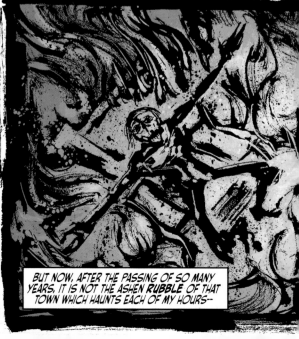

BUT NOW, AFTER THE PASSING OF SO MANY
YEARS, IT IS NOT THE ASHEN **RUBBLE** OF THAT
TOWN WHICH HAUNTS EACH OF MY HOURS--

--IT IS THAT ONE GREAT **RUIN** IN WHOSE **SHADOW** MY MIND HAS BEEN INTERNED.
THE END

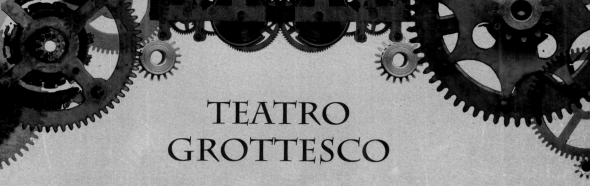

TEATRO GROTTESCO

If all the world's a stage, as that bard guy and practically everyone else has said, then its play-book overflows with Grand Guignol and grotesquerie. Nor should we overlook that its actors—us, that is—must at some point all star in scenes of ravaging mayhem and boundless nightmare. And everyone dies in the end. Had we not all been born on the very boards of this dreadful playhouse, one can only wonder what idiot would choose to join the company of the doomed.

No one knows who or what is behind the *Teatro Grottesco*, that is, our world theater. But whoever or whatever it is seems to get off on staging the cruel mise-en-scène of what we like to call "life," which is a complete construct of our heads and not anything guided by a coherent plot. The *Teatro Grottesco* does not go in for coherence. Its genre is disorder, a chaotic succession of derangements and deformations.

Nevertheless, it must be admitted that some seasons of the Teatro are worse than others. Sometimes we may even lie back with a cool drink in hand and exclaim, "Man, this is the life." On such occasions, we can be positive we have missed something crucial to the Teatro's scheme. That something is *anxiety*. Whenever we are not immediately enmeshed in some horror or another, we should be on the lookout for one. If we are alert, and not lolling in a false sense of serenity, we should be properly anxious. More appropriately, we should be sick with disquietude, brooding with qualms, and jumpy with anticipation for the next freak lurking in the shadows, waiting to sidle up to us when we least expect it. Because we can never be sure that the Teatro is not already in town, or at least waiting on the outskirts of where we live. Therefore, anxiety is the only tune that rings true in our lives, which is to say, that stagy world that is owned and operated by the *Teatro Grottesco*.

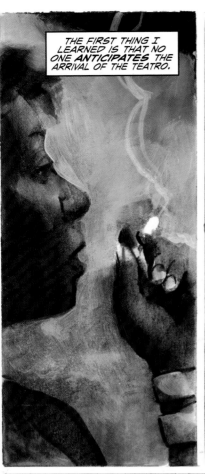

THE FIRST THING I LEARNED IS THAT NO ONE *ANTICIPATES* THE ARRIVAL OF THE TEATRO.

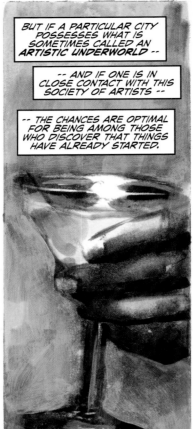

BUT IF A PARTICULAR CITY POSSESSES WHAT IS SOMETIMES CALLED AN *ARTISTIC UNDERWORLD* --

-- AND IF ONE IS IN CLOSE CONTACT WITH THIS SOCIETY OF ARTISTS --

-- THE CHANCES ARE OPTIMAL FOR BEING AMONG THOSE WHO DISCOVER THAT THINGS HAVE ALREADY STARTED.

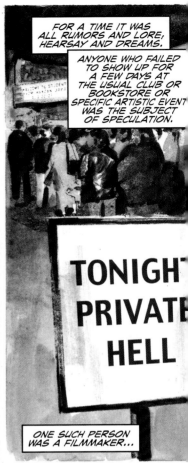

FOR A TIME IT WAS ALL RUMORS AND LORE, HEARSAY AND DREAMS.

ANYONE WHO FAILED TO SHOW UP FOR A FEW DAYS AT THE USUAL CLUB OR BOOKSTORE OR SPECIFIC ARTISTIC EVENT WAS THE SUBJECT OF SPECULATION.

TONIGH
PRIVATE
HELL

ONE SUCH PERSON WAS A FILMMAKER...

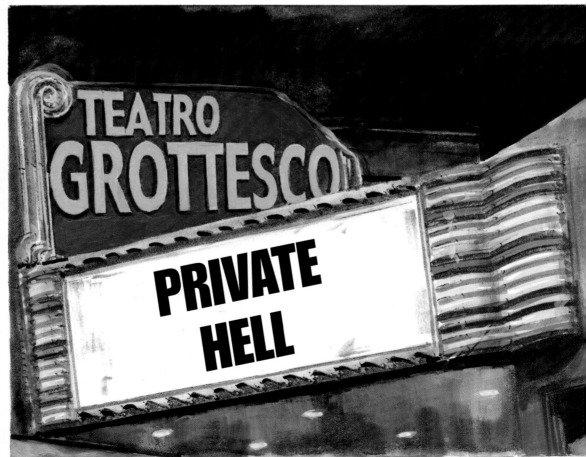

TEATRO GROTTESCO

PRIVATE HELL

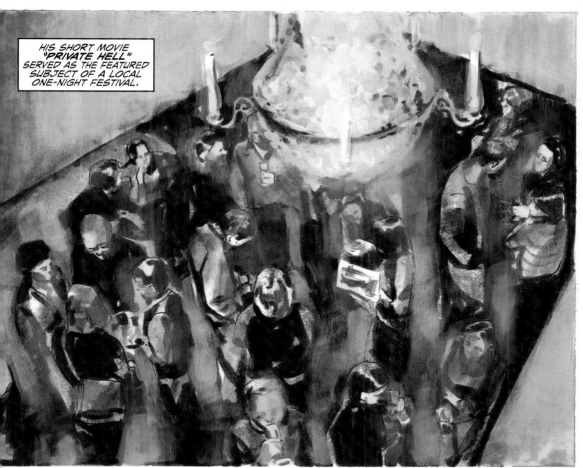

HIS SHORT MOVIE *"PRIVATE HELL"* SERVED AS THE FEATURED SUBJECT OF A LOCAL ONE-NIGHT FESTIVAL.

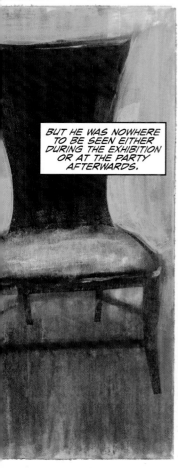

BUT HE WAS NOWHERE TO BE SEEN EITHER DURING THE EXHIBITION OR AT THE PARTY AFTERWARDS.

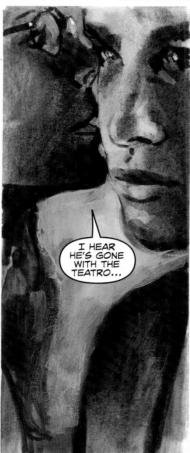

I HEAR HE'S GONE WITH THE TEATRO...

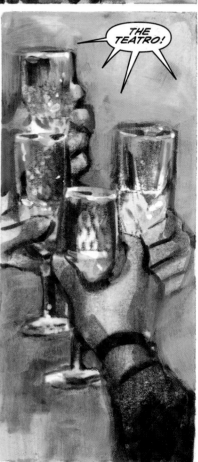

THE TEATRO!

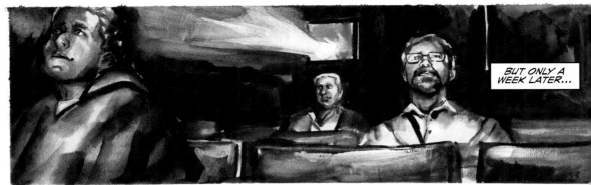

BUT ONLY A WEEK LATER...

THE FILMMAKER WAS SPOTTED IN THE BACK ROW OF A PORNOGRAPHIC THEATER.

HE LATER EXPLAINED HIS ABSENCE BY EXPLAINING HE HAD BEEN IN THE HOSPITAL FOLLOWING A THOROUGH BEATING AT THE HANDS OF SOME PEOPLE HE HAD BEEN FILMING WHO DID NOT CONSENT OR DESIRE TO BE *FILMED.*

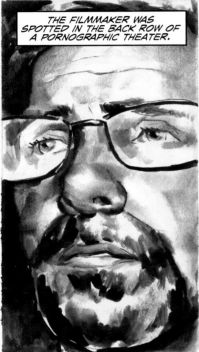

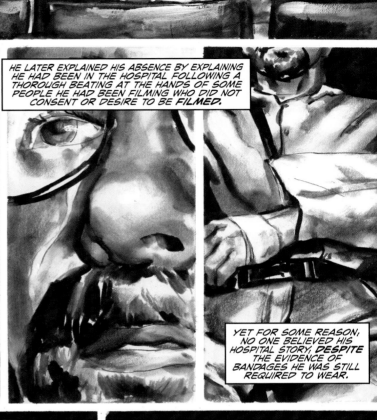

YET FOR SOME REASON, NO ONE BELIEVED HIS HOSPITAL STORY, *DESPITE* THE EVIDENCE OF BANDAGES HE WAS STILL REQUIRED TO WEAR.

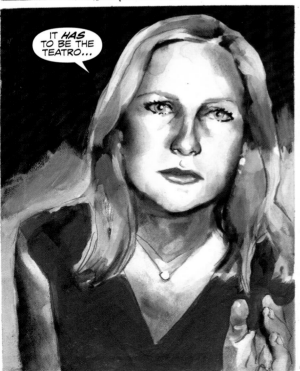

IT *HAS* TO BE THE TEATRO...

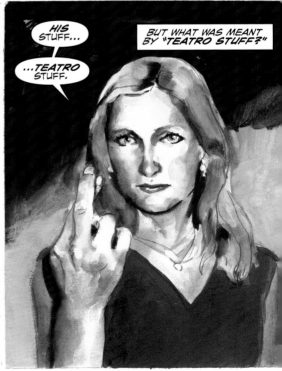

HIS STUFF...

...TEATRO STUFF.

BUT WHAT WAS MEANT BY *"TEATRO STUFF?"*

CERTAINLY THERE IS NO SHORTAGE OF ANECDOTES THAT HAVE BEEN PASSED AROUND WHICH PURPORT TO ILLUMINATE THE NATURE AND WORKINGS OF THIS *CRUEL TROUPE* --

AN EPITHET USED BY THOSE WHO ARE TOO SUPERSTITIOUS TO INVOKE THE *TEATRO GROTTESCO* BY NAME.

BUT SORTING OUT THESE ACCOUNTS INTO A COHERENT *PROFILE* -- NEVER MIND THEIR TRUTH VALUE -- IS ANOTHER THING ENTIRELY.

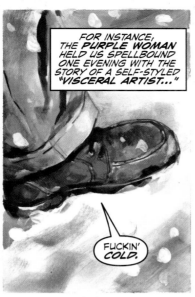

FOR INSTANCE, THE *PURPLE WOMAN* HELD US SPELLBOUND ONE EVENING WITH THE STORY OF A SELF-STYLED *"VISCERAL ARTIST..."*

FUCKIN' *COLD.*

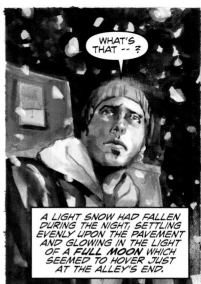

WHAT'S THAT -- ?

A LIGHT SNOW HAD FALLEN DURING THE NIGHT, SETTLING EVENLY UPON THE PAVEMENT AND GLOWING IN THE LIGHT OF A *FULL MOON* WHICH SEEMED TO HOVER JUST AT THE ALLEY'S END.

THE ARTIST SAW A *FIGURE* IN THE DISTANCE, AND SOMETHING *ABOUT* THIS FIGURE MADE HIM PAUSE FOR A MOMENT AND STARE.

ALTHOUGH HE HAD A TRAINED EYE FOR SIZING AND PERSPECTIVE...HE COULD NOT TELL IF IT WAS SHORT OR TALL, OR EVEN IF IT WAS MOVING OR STANDING STILL.

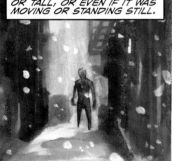

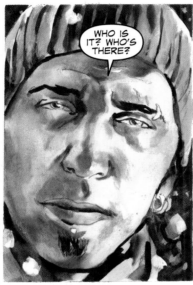

WHO IS IT? WHO'S THERE?

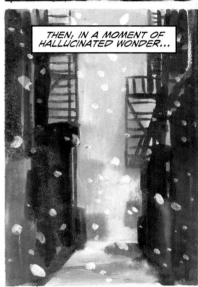

THEN, IN A MOMENT OF HALLUCINATED WONDER...

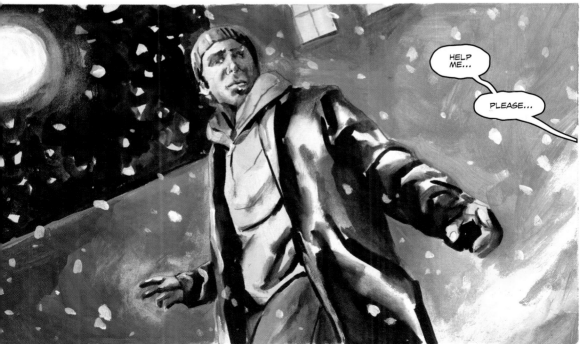

HELP ME...

PLEASE...

I CANNOT KEEP THEM AWAY FROM ME ANYMORE...
PLEASE...
I AM BECOMING SO SMALL...
...AND WEAK...
MY GOD...
IN HIS POCKET, THE ARTIST HAD A TOOL WHICH HE USED FOR CUTTING OPEN BOXES AT HIS SUPERMARKET JOB.
HE HAD CUT INTO FLESH IN THE PAST.
UNDER THE CIRCUMSTANCES, WHAT HE HAD DONE SEEMED PERFECTLY JUSTIFIED TO THE ARTIST.
THE MAN WAS BECOMING SO SMALL.

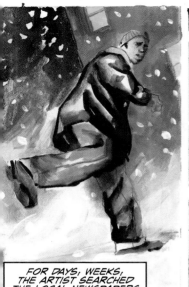

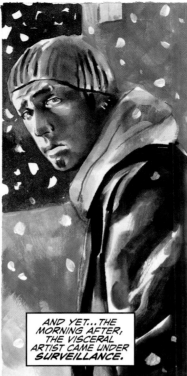

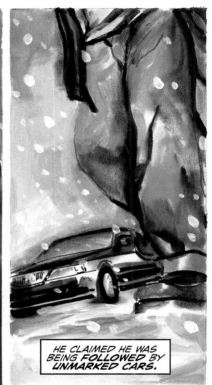

FOR DAYS, WEEKS, THE ARTIST SEARCHED THE LOCAL NEWSPAPERS FOR SOME WORD OF THE *EXTRAORDINARY* THING THE *POLICE* MUST HAVE FOUND IN THAT ALLEY.

BUT NOTHING EVER APPEARED.

AND YET...THE MORNING AFTER, THE *VISCERAL* ARTIST CAME UNDER *SURVEILLANCE*.

HE CLAIMED HE WAS BEING *FOLLOWED* BY *UNMARKED CARS*.

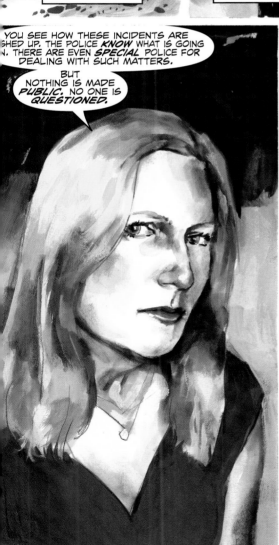

YOU SEE HOW THESE INCIDENTS ARE [HUS]HED UP. THE POLICE *KNOW* WHAT IS GOING [O]N. THERE ARE EVEN *SPECIAL* POLICE FOR DEALING WITH SUCH MATTERS.

BUT NOTHING IS MADE *PUBLIC*. NO ONE IS *QUESTIONED*.

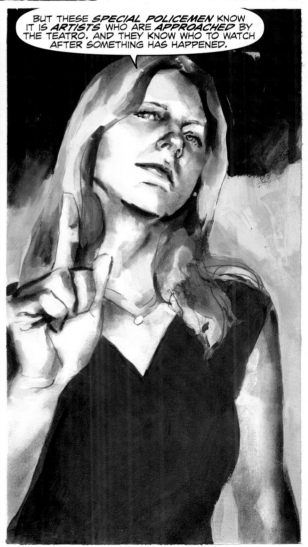

BUT THESE *SPECIAL POLICEMEN* KNOW IT IS *ARTISTS* WHO ARE *APPROACHED* BY THE *TEATRO*. AND THEY KNOW WHO TO WATCH AFTER SOMETHING HAS HAPPENED.

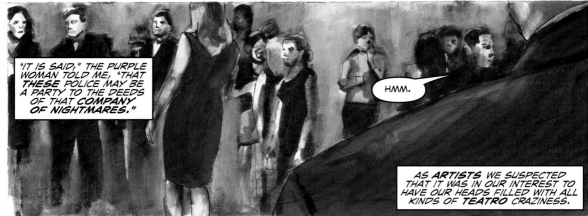

"IT IS SAID," THE PURPLE WOMAN TOLD ME, "THAT *THESE* POLICE MAY BE A PARTY TO THE DEEDS OF THAT *COMPANY OF NIGHTMARES.*"

HMM.

AS *ARTISTS* WE SUSPECTED THAT IT WAS IN OUR INTEREST TO HAVE OUR HEADS FILLED WITH ALL KINDS OF *TEATRO* CRAZINESS.

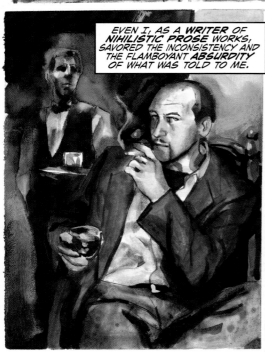

EVEN I, AS A *WRITER* OF *NIHILISTIC PROSE* WORKS, SAVORED THE INCONSISTENCY AND THE FLAMBOYANT *ABSURDITY* OF WHAT WAS TOLD TO ME.

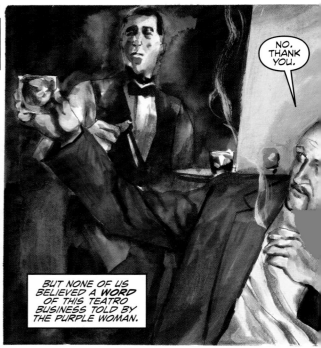

NO. THANK YOU.

BUT NONE OF US BELIEVED A *WORD* OF THIS TEATRO BUSINESS TOLD BY THE PURPLE WOMAN.

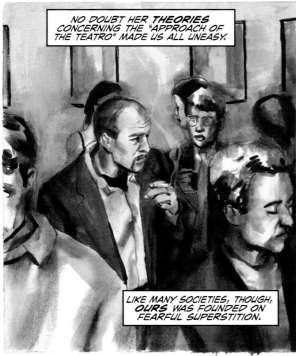

NO DOUBT HER *THEORIES* CONCERNING THE "APPROACH OF THE TEATRO" MADE US ALL UNEASY.

LIKE MANY SOCIETIES, THOUGH, *OURS* WAS FOUNDED ON FEARFUL SUPERSTITION.

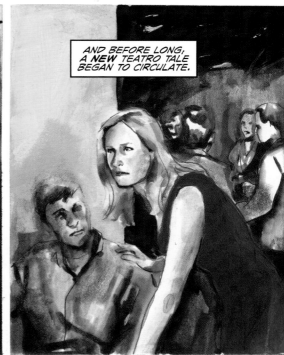

AND BEFORE LONG, A *NEW* TEATRO TALE BEGAN TO CIRCULATE.

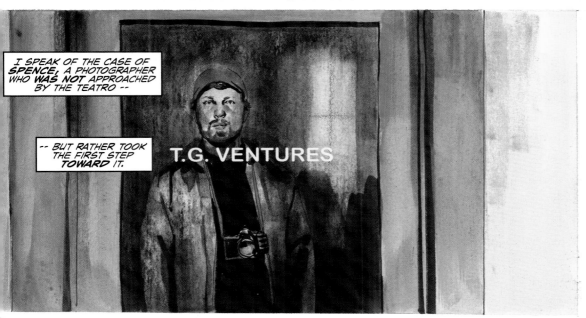

I SPEAK OF THE CASE OF **SPENCE**, A PHOTOGRAPHER WHO **WAS NOT** APPROACHED BY THE TEATRO --

-- BUT RATHER TOOK THE FIRST STEP **TOWARD** IT.

T.G. VENTURES

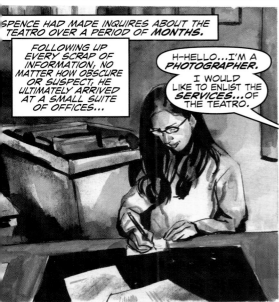

SPENCE HAD MADE INQUIRES ABOUT THE TEATRO OVER A PERIOD OF **MONTHS.**

FOLLOWING UP EVERY SCRAP OF INFORMATION, NO MATTER HOW OBSCURE OR SUSPECT, HE ULTIMATELY ARRIVED AT A SMALL SUITE OF OFFICES...

H-HELLO...I'M A **PHOTOGRAPHER.** I WOULD LIKE TO ENLIST THE **SERVICES**...OF THE TEATRO.

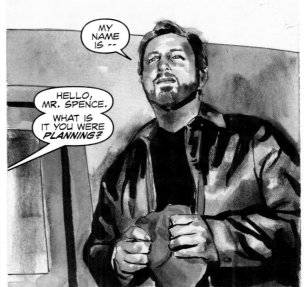

MY NAME IS --

HELLO, MR. SPENCE. WHAT IS IT YOU WERE **PLANNING?**

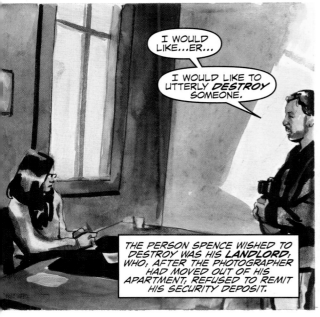

I WOULD LIKE...ER...

I WOULD LIKE TO UTTERLY **DESTROY** SOMEONE.

THE PERSON SPENCE WISHED TO DESTROY WAS HIS **LANDLORD,** WHO, AFTER THE PHOTOGRAPHER HAD MOVED OUT OF HIS APARTMENT, REFUSED TO REMIT HIS SECURITY DEPOSIT.

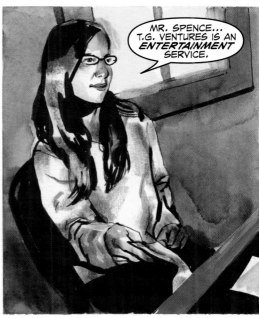

MR. SPENCE... T.G. VENTURES IS AN **ENTERTAINMENT** SERVICE.

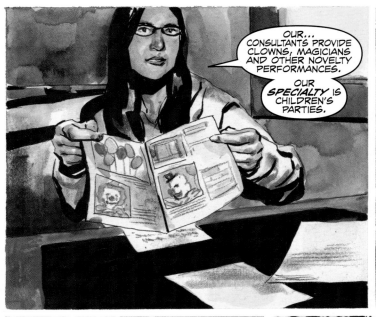

OUR... CONSULTANTS PROVIDE CLOWNS, MAGICIANS AND OTHER NOVELTY PERFORMANCES.

OUR *SPECIALTY* IS CHILDREN'S PARTIES.

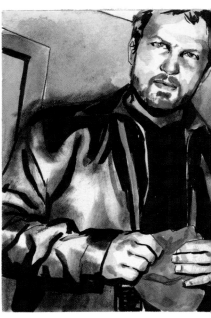

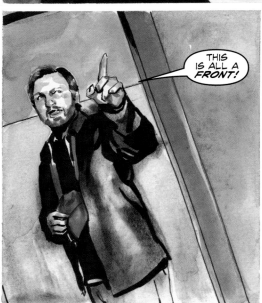

THIS IS ALL A *FRONT!*

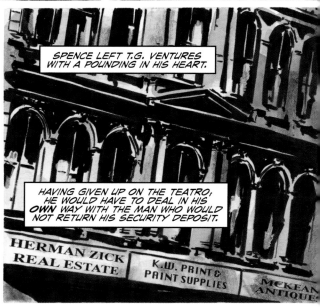

SPENCE LEFT T.G. VENTURES WITH A POUNDING IN HIS HEART.

HAVING GIVEN UP ON THE TEATRO, HE WOULD HAVE TO DEAL IN HIS *OWN* WAY WITH THE MAN WHO WOULD NOT RETURN HIS SECURITY DEPOSIT.

HERMAN ZICK REAL ESTATE

K.W. PRINT & PAINT SUPPLIES

McKEAN ANTIQUE

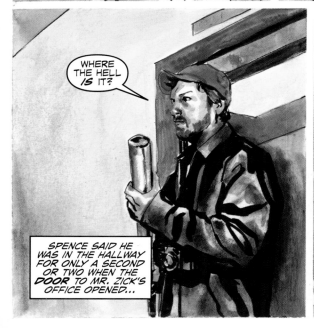

WHERE THE HELL *IS* IT?

SPENCE SAID HE WAS IN THE HALLWAY FOR ONLY A SECOND OR TWO WHEN THE *DOOR* TO MR. ZICK'S OFFICE OPENED...

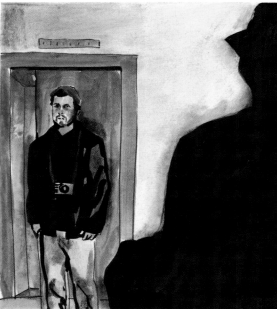

EXCUSE ME, DO YOU KNOW WHERE I CAN FIND --
T.G.V.
A SPLIT-SECOND BEFORE THE ELEVATOR DOORS SLID CLOSED, THE GENTLEMAN LOOKED AT SPENCE...
CLIK

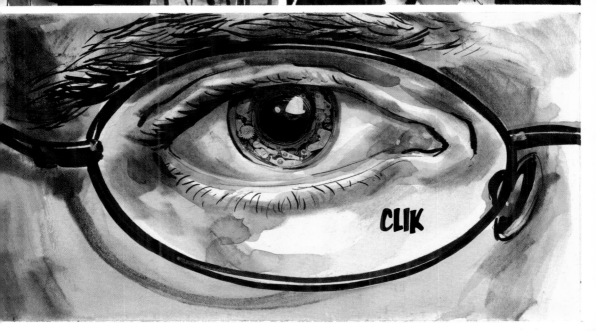

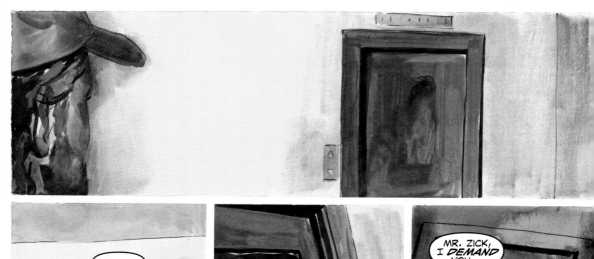

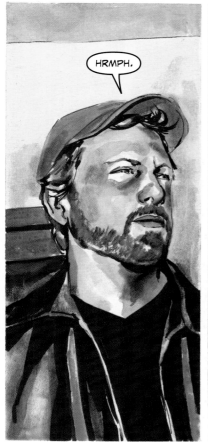

HRMPH.

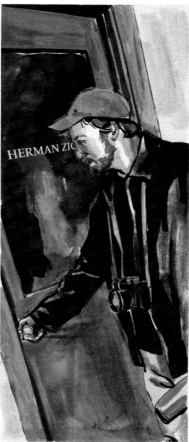

HERMAN ZIC

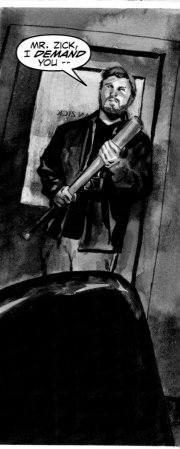

MR. ZICK, I *DEMAND* YOU --

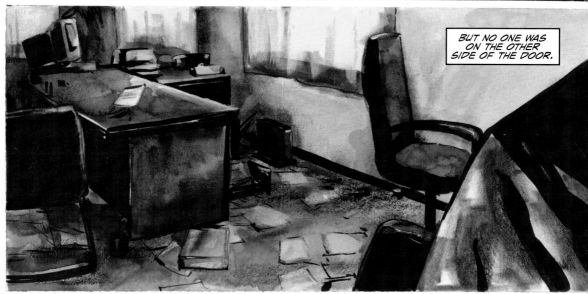

BUT NO ONE WAS ON THE OTHER SIDE OF THE DOOR.

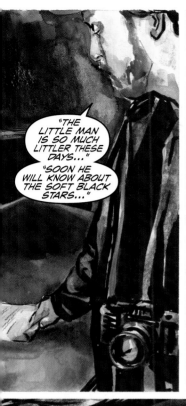

"THE LITTLE MAN IS SO MUCH LITTLER THESE DAYS..."

"SOON HE WILL KNOW ABOUT THE SOFT BLACK STARS..."

man is so much these days... he will know about the soft black stars... And your PAYMENT is past due.

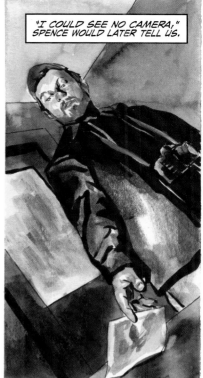

"I COULD SEE NO CAMERA," SPENCE WOULD LATER TELL US.

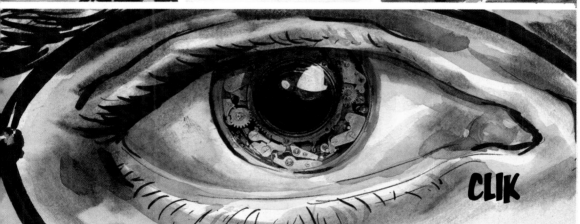

CLIK

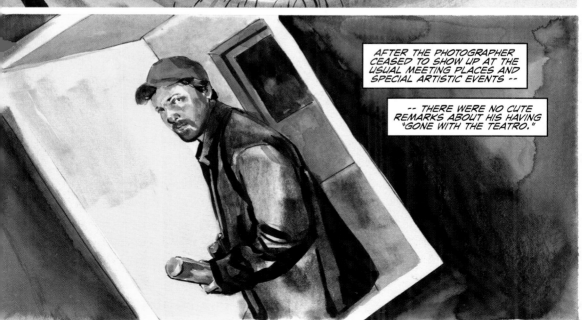

AFTER THE PHOTOGRAPHER CEASED TO SHOW UP AT THE USUAL MEETING PLACES AND SPECIAL ARTISTIC EVENTS --

-- THERE WERE NO CUTE REMARKS ABOUT HIS HAVING "GONE WITH THE TEATRO."

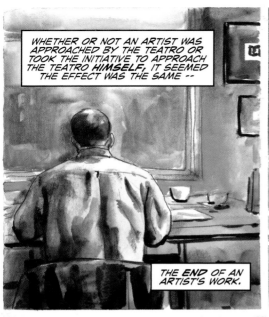

WHETHER OR NOT AN ARTIST WAS APPROACHED BY THE TEATRO OR TOOK THE INITIATIVE TO APPROACH THE TEATRO *HIMSELF*, IT SEEMED THE EFFECT WAS THE SAME --

THE *END* OF AN ARTIST'S WORK.

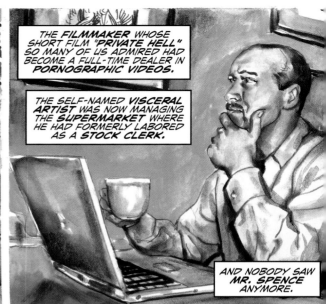

THE *FILMMAKER* WHOSE SHORT FILM *"PRIVATE HELL"* SO MANY OF US ADMIRED HAD BECOME A FULL-TIME DEALER IN *PORNOGRAPHIC VIDEOS*.

THE SELF-NAMED *VISCERAL ARTIST* WAS NOW MANAGING THE *SUPERMARKET* WHERE HE HAD FORMERLY LABORED AS A *STOCK CLERK*.

AND NOBODY SAW *MR. SPENCE* ANYMORE.

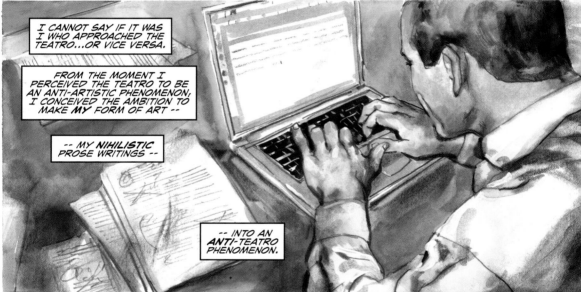

I CANNOT SAY IF IT WAS I WHO APPROACHED THE TEATRO...OR VICE VERSA.

FROM THE MOMENT I PERCEIVED THE TEATRO TO BE AN ANTI-ARTISTIC PHENOMENON, I CONCEIVED THE AMBITION TO MAKE *MY* FORM OF ART --

-- MY *NIHILISTIC* PROSE WRITINGS --

-- INTO AN *ANTI-TEATRO* PHENOMENON.

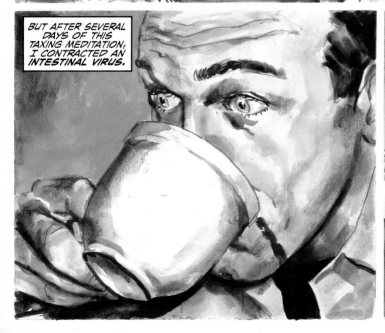

BUT AFTER SEVERAL DAYS OF THIS TAXING MEDITATION, I CONTRACTED AN *INTESTINAL VIRUS*.

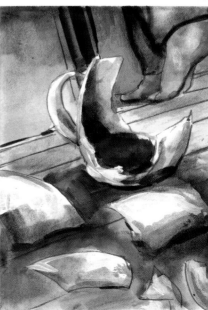

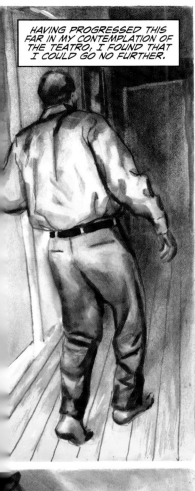

HAVING PROGRESSED THIS FAR IN MY CONTEMPLATION OF THE TEATRO, I FOUND THAT I COULD GO NO FURTHER.

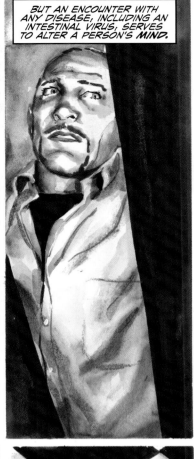

BUT AN ENCOUNTER WITH ANY DISEASE, INCLUDING AN INTESTINAL VIRUS, SERVES TO ALTER A PERSON'S **MIND.**

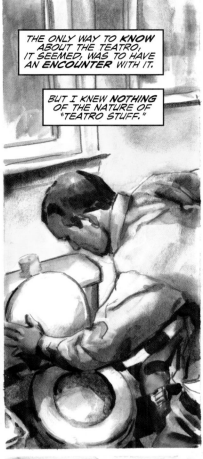

THE ONLY WAY TO **KNOW** ABOUT THE TEATRO, IT SEEMED, WAS TO HAVE AN **ENCOUNTER** WITH IT.

BUT I KNEW **NOTHING** OF THE NATURE OF "TEATRO STUFF."

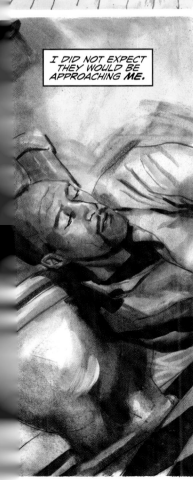

I DID NOT EXPECT THEY WOULD BE APPROACHING **ME.**

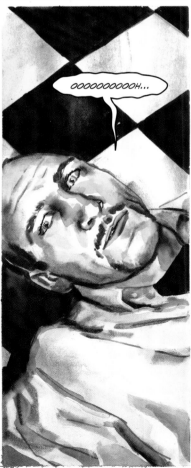

OOOOOOOOOOH...

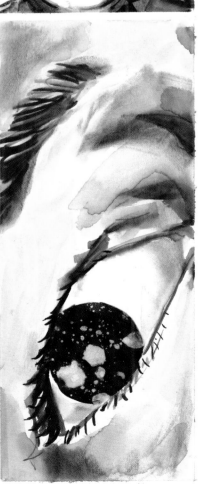

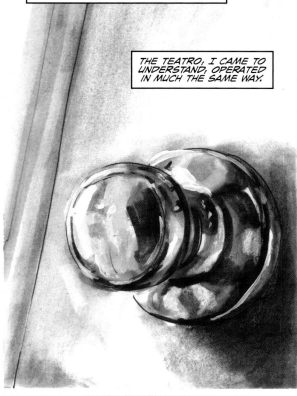

SUFFERING THROUGH THE MANY DAYS AND NIGHTS OF AN INTESTINAL VIRUS, ONE BECOMES HIGHLY CONSCIOUS OF CERTAIN **REALITIES.**

THE TEATRO, I CAME TO UNDERSTAND, OPERATED IN MUCH THE SAME WAY.

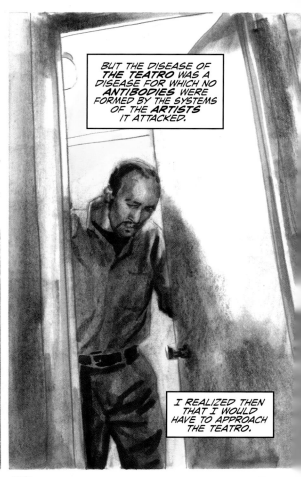

BUT THE DISEASE OF **THE TEATRO** WAS A DISEASE FOR WHICH NO **ANTIBODIES** WERE FORMED BY THE SYSTEMS OF THE **ARTISTS** IT ATTACKED.

I REALIZED THEN THAT I WOULD HAVE TO APPROACH THE TEATRO.

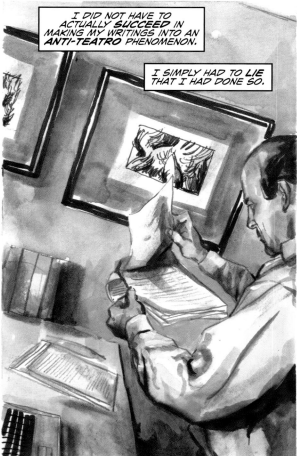

I DID NOT HAVE TO ACTUALLY **SUCCEED** IN MAKING MY WRITINGS INTO AN **ANTI-TEATRO** PHENOMENON.

I SIMPLY HAD TO **LIE** THAT I HAD DONE SO.

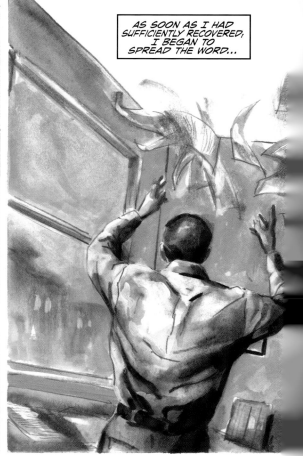

AS SOON AS I HAD SUFFICIENTLY RECOVERED, I BEGAN TO SPREAD THE WORD...

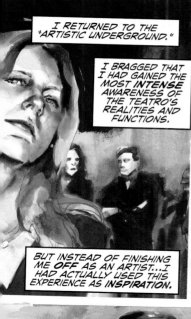

I RETURNED TO THE "ARTISTIC UNDERGROUND."

I BRAGGED THAT I HAD GAINED THE MOST *INTENSE* AWARENESS OF THE *TEATRO'S* REALITIES AND FUNCTIONS.

BUT INSTEAD OF FINISHING ME *OFF* AS AN ARTIST...I HAD ACTUALLY USED THIS EXPERIENCE AS *INSPIRATION.*

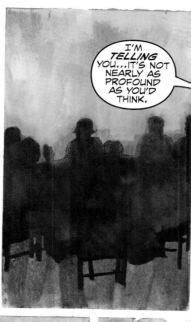

I'M *TELLING* YOU...IT'S NOT NEARLY AS PROFOUND AS YOU'D THINK.

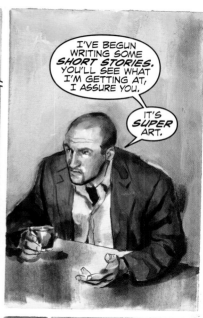

I'VE BEGUN WRITING SOME *SHORT STORIES.* YOU'LL SEE WHAT I'M GETTING AT, I ASSURE YOU.

IT'S *SUPER* ART.

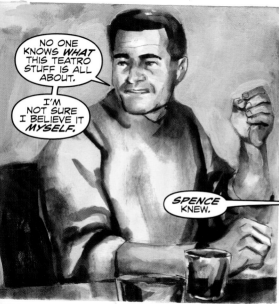

NO ONE KNOWS *WHAT* THIS TEATRO STUFF IS ALL ABOUT.

I'M NOT SURE I BELIEVE IT *MYSELF.*

SPENCE KNEW.

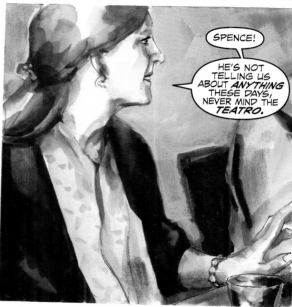

SPENCE!

HE'S NOT TELLING US ABOUT *ANYTHING* THESE DAYS, NEVER MIND THE *TEATRO.*

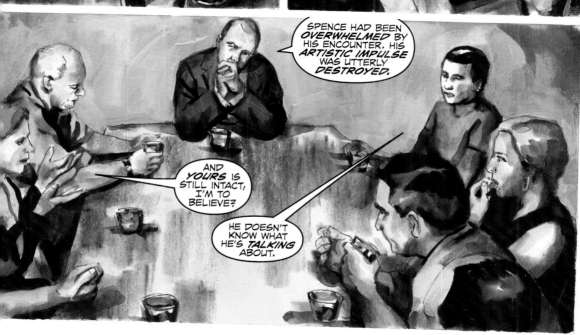

SPENCE HAD BEEN *OVERWHELMED* BY HIS ENCOUNTER. HIS *ARTISTIC IMPULSE* WAS UTTERLY *DESTROYED.*

AND *YOURS* IS STILL INTACT, I'M TO BELIEVE?

HE DOESN'T KNOW WHAT HE'S *TALKING* ABOUT.

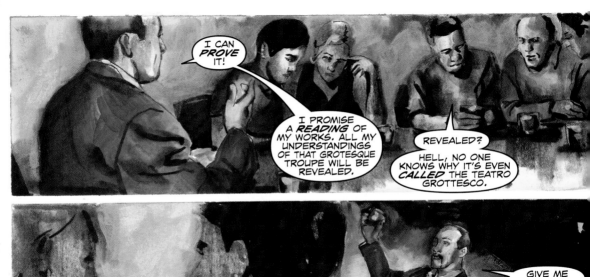

I CAN **PROVE** IT!

I PROMISE A **READING** OF MY WORKS. ALL MY UNDERSTANDINGS OF THAT GROTESQUE TROUPE WILL BE REVEALED.

REVEALED? HELL, NO ONE KNOWS WHY IT'S EVEN **CALLED** THE TEATRO GROTTESCO.

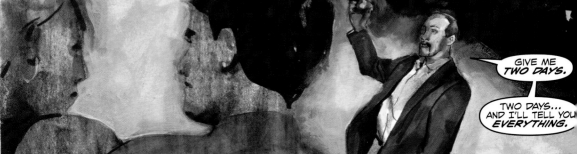

GIVE ME **TWO DAYS**.

TWO DAYS... AND I'LL TELL YOU **EVERYTHING**.

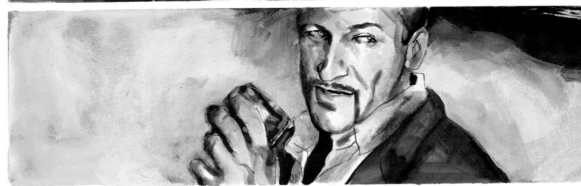

TWO DAYS.

WITHIN THAT PERIOD OF TIME, I KNEW I WOULD EITHER HAVE **SUCCEEDED** OR **FAILED** TO PROVOKE AN ENCOUNTER WITH THE TEATRO..

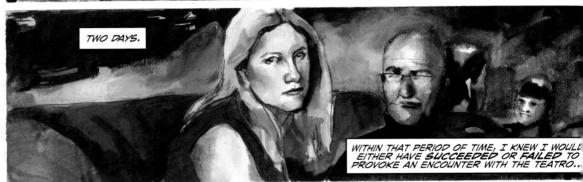

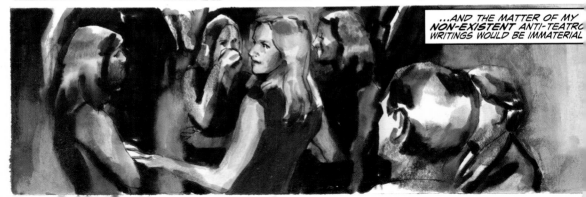

...AND THE MATTER OF MY **NON-EXISTENT** ANTI-TEATRO WRITINGS WOULD BE IMMATERIAL

THE NEXT DAY, HOWEVER, I COLLAPSED DURING A CONVERSATION WITH A DIFFERENT CONGREGATION OF ARTISTS...
DES ESSEINTES' LIBRARY
ALTHOUGH THE SYMPTOMS OF MY INTESTINAL VIRUS HAD NEVER ENTIRELY DISAPPEARED, I HAD NOT EXPECTED TO COLLAPSE THE WAY I DID.
I HAD NOT EXPECTED TO DISCOVER WHAT I THOUGHT WAS AN INTESTINAL VIRUS WAS SOMETHING FAR MORE SERIOUS.

WHEN I AWOKE, I FELT NONE OF THE PAIN THAT HAD CAUSED ME TO COLLAPSE.
AT THAT MOMENT I COULD FEEL NOTHING OF THE EXPERIENCES OF MY PAST LIFE. IT SEEMED I HAD ALWAYS BEEN AN OCCUPANT OF THAT DARK HOSPITAL WARD --
-- AND ALWAYS WOULD BE.
I SAT THERE AT THE EDGE OF THE MATTRESS FOR A QUITE A WHILE BEFORE --
PAGING DR. GRODDECK...
...*KSSH*... DR. GRODDECK...PAGING DR. GRODDECK...

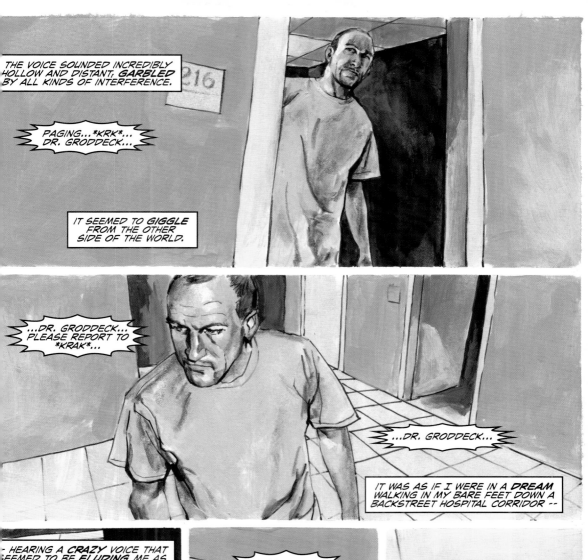

THE VOICE SOUNDED INCREDIBLY HOLLOW AND DISTANT, *GARBLED* BY ALL KINDS OF INTERFERENCE.

PAGING...*KRK*... DR. GRODDECK...

IT SEEMED TO *GIGGLE* FROM THE OTHER SIDE OF THE WORLD.

...DR. GRODDECK... PLEASE REPORT TO *KRAK*...

...DR. GRODDECK...

IT WAS AS IF I WERE IN A *DREAM* WALKING IN MY BARE FEET DOWN A BACKSTREET HOSPITAL CORRIDOR --

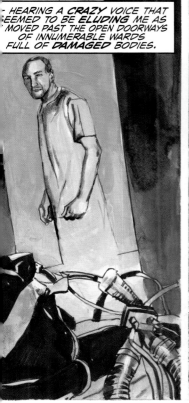

-- HEARING A *CRAZY* VOICE THAT SEEMED TO BE *ELUDING* ME AS I MOVED PAST THE OPEN DOORWAYS OF INNUMERABLE WARDS FULL OF *DAMAGED* BODIES.

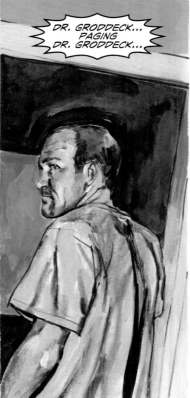

DR. GRODDECK... PAGING DR. GRODDECK...

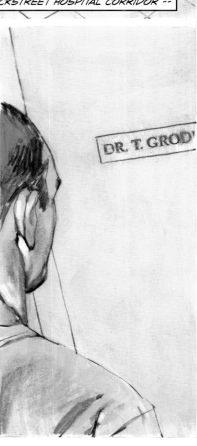

DR. T. GROD

I'M PLEASED TO FINALLY MEET YOU IN *PERSON.*
THERE IS AN *OPENING* IN OUR ORGANIZATION FOR SOMEONE WITH YOUR RESOURCEFULNESS AND IMAGINATION.
COME.
COME AND SEE.

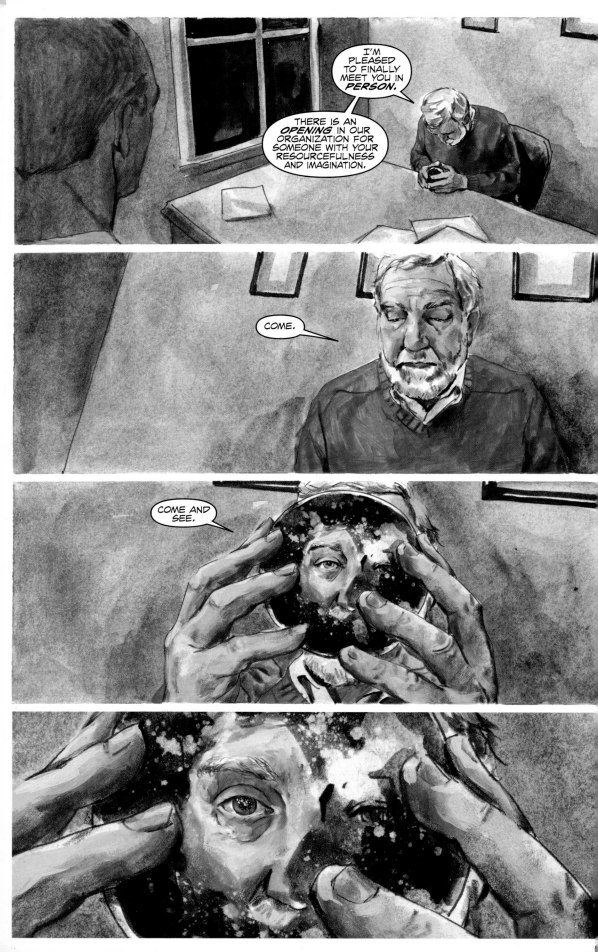

AS YOU MIGHT HAVE NOTICED BY NOW, ALL THIS *ARTISTIC* BUSINESS CAN ONLY KEEP YOU GOING SO *LONG.*
I WAS FORCED INTO THE REALIZATION *MYSELF* ONCE... AND I'M QUITE MINDFUL OF WHAT A *BLOW* IT CAN BE.
BY THE WAY, THE RESULTS OF YOUR *TESTS* ARE GOING TO COME BACK *POSITIVE.*
IF YOU THINK AN *INTESTINAL VIRUS* IS MISERY, JUST WAIT A FEW MORE MONTHS.
I REALIZED THAT THERE IS SUCH A THING AS BEING APPROACHED IN ORDER TO *FORCE* ONE'S HAND INTO MAKING WHAT ONLY *APPEARS* TO BE AN APPROACH --
-- WHICH IS ACTUALLY A *NON-APPROACH* THAT NEGATES THE WHOLE CONCEPT OF APPROACHING.
IT WAS ALL A FIX FROM THE START BECAUSE I BELONGED TO AN *ARTISTIC UNDERWORLD.*
BECAUSE I WAS AN ARTIST WHOSE *WORK* WOULD BE BROUGHT TO AN *END* BY AN ENCOUNTER WITH THE *TEATRO GROTTESCO.*

YOU SHOULD BE PROUD THAT WE HAVE A SPECIAL PART FOR YOU TO PLAY, SUCH A TALENTED ARTIST.
WE WILL ARRANGE ANOTHER MEETING WITH YOU IN ANY CASE.
AND REMEMBER --
-- YOU APPROACHED US.

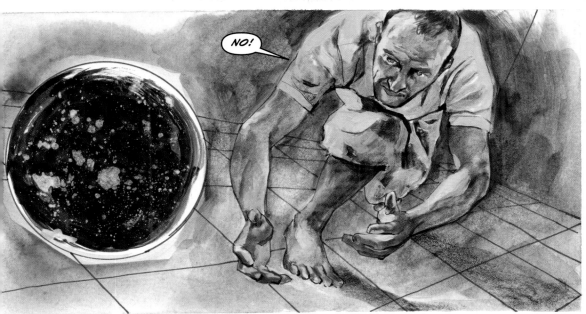

NO!

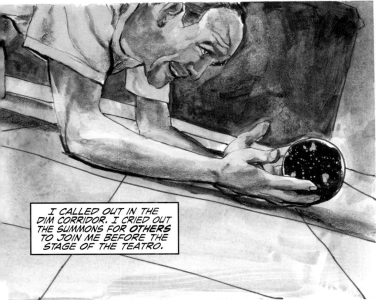

I CALLED OUT IN THE DIM CORRIDOR. I CRIED OUT THE SUMMONS FOR *OTHERS* TO JOIN ME BEFORE THE STAGE OF THE TEATRO.

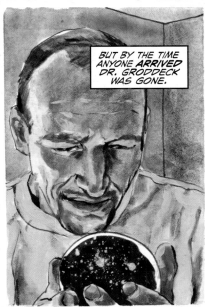

BUT BY THE TIME ANYONE *ARRIVED* DR. GRODDECK WAS GONE.

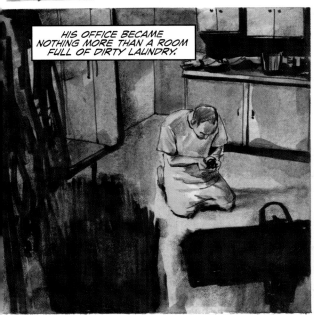

HIS OFFICE BECAME NOTHING MORE THAN A ROOM FULL OF DIRTY LAUNDRY.

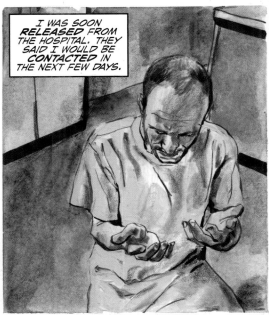

I WAS SOON *RELEASED* FROM THE HOSPITAL. THEY SAID I WOULD BE *CONTACTED* IN THE NEXT FEW DAYS.

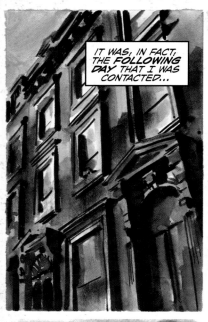

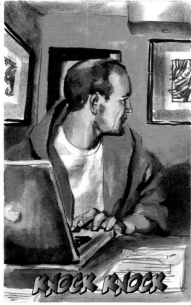

IT WAS, IN FACT, THE **FOLLOWING DAY** THAT I WAS CONTACTED...

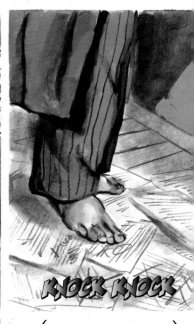

KNOCK KNOCK

KNOCK KNOCK

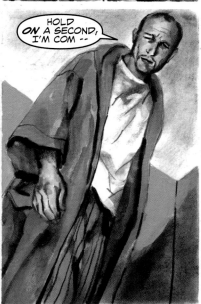

HOLD **ON** A SECOND, I'M COM --

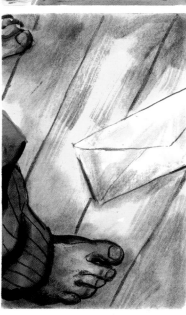

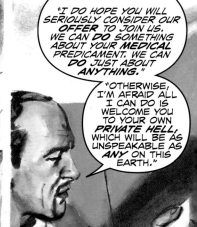

"I DO HOPE YOU WILL SERIOUSLY CONSIDER OUR **OFFER** TO JOIN US. WE CAN **DO SOMETHING** ABOUT YOUR **MEDICAL** PREDICAMENT. WE CAN **DO JUST ABOUT ANYTHING**."

"OTHERWISE, I'M AFRAID ALL I CAN DO IS WELCOME YOU TO YOUR OWN **PRIVATE HELL**, WHICH WILL BE AS UNSPEAKABLE AS **ANY** ON THIS EARTH."

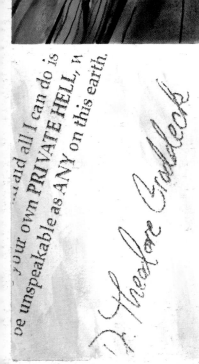

...raid all I can do is ...your own PRIVATE HELL, ...e unspeakable as ANY on this earth.

D. Theodore Graddeck

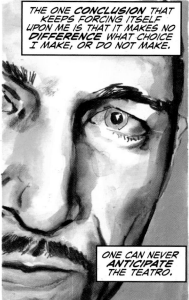

THE ONE **CONCLUSION** THAT KEEPS FORCING ITSELF UPON ME IS THAT IT MAKES NO **DIFFERENCE** WHAT CHOICE I MAKE, OR DO NOT MAKE.

ONE CAN NEVER **ANTICIPATE** THE TEATRO.

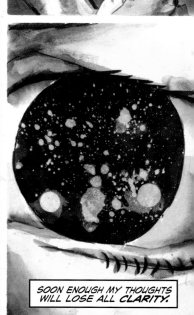

SOON ENOUGH MY THOUGHTS WILL LOSE ALL **CLARITY**.

THE SOFT BLACK STARS HAVE ALREADY BEGUN TO FILL THE SKY.
THE END

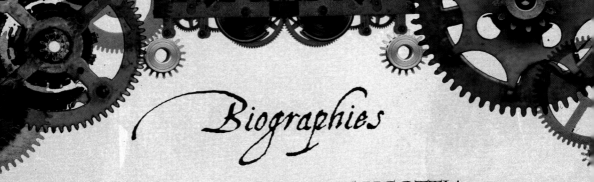

Biographies

Something of a cult figure, THOMAS LIGOTTI is comparatively little known, but has been bestowed high praise as one of the most effective and unique horror writers of recent decades. Often compared to writers such as Edgar Allan Poe, Jorge Luis Borges, Franz Kafka, and H. P. Lovecraft, Ligotti has been called "the best kept secret in contemporary horror fiction" by none other than the *Washington Post*.

Brooklyn-based STUART MOORE's recent writing includes the graphic novel series *Earthlight* (Tokyopop), *New Avengers/Transformers* (Marvel Comics), *Firestorm* (DC Comics), the original science-fiction series *PARA* (Penny-Farthing Press), a graphic novel adaptation of the bestselling fantasy novel *Redwall* (Penguin/Philomel), and the prose novels *American Meat* and *Reality Bites* (Games Workshop). He won the Will Eisner Award for Best Editor in 1996.

JOE HARRIS is a horror screenwriter, filmmaker, and comic book creator. His feature screenplay debut, *Darkness Falls*, was based on *Tooth Fairy*, a short film which he directed. *The Tripper*, a politically themed slasher film cowritten by Harris and actor David Arquette, was released in theaters in 2007. Joe lives in New York City, home of superheroes, beautiful women, and his beloved New York Yankees.

COLLEEN DORAN has worked at Disney, Marvel Comics, DC Comics, Image, Lucasfilm, Dark Horse, Sony, and Scholastic. Credits include *Spider-Man*, *The Sandman*, *Wonder Woman*, *A Distant Soil*, *Walt Disney's Beauty and the Beast*, *Clive Barker's Hellraiser*, and others. She has been an artist in residence at the Smithsonian Institute and has received many awards and honors for her work. She lives on a mountain in the middle of nowhere.

BEN TEMPLESMITH is a commercial illustrator and multiple Eisner Award nominee who can be found at templesmith.com. When he's not eating babies he works on the critically acclaimed *Fell* with Warren Ellis, as well as *Wormwood: Gentleman Corpse* and *30 Days of Night: Red Snow*, both of which he writes and draws himself at his studio in Perth, Australia, where he attempts in vain to get what those in the "industry" call "sleep" at least a couple hours a day. Ben lives in the future, being around sixteen hours ahead of American time zones.

TED McKEEVER's graphic style is extremely distinct, drawn in bold, angular lines that give his work a fantastic edge. He's also known for his unique, ambitious, and emotionally dynamic writing. Ted jumped into the comics scene in 1986 with his B&W works *Transit* and *Eddy Current*, the latter bringing Eisner Award nominations. Later works include everything from *Batman* to *The Matrix*, as well as his own *Metropol* and *Faith*.

MICHAEL GAYDOS is a draftsman, painter, and printmaker who has worked for Marvel Comics, DC Comics, Image, Dark Horse, Fox Atomic, Tundra, NBM, Caliber, and White Wolf, among others. He has received two Eisner Award nominations for his work on *Alias* with Brian Michael Bendis for Marvel. Michael lives and works in Warwick, New York.

ASHLEY WOOD draws and paints . . . likes robots and cats.

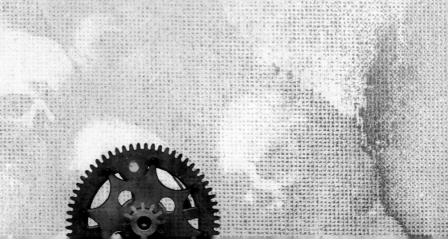